THE EASTERN QUESTION

STUDIES IN HISTORY, ECONOMICS AND PUBLIC LAW

EDITED BY THE FACULTY OF POLITICAL SCIENCE OF
COLUMBIA UNIVERSITY

Volume XIV]   [Number 3

THE
EASTERN QUESTION
A STUDY IN DIPLOMACY

BY

STEPHEN PIERCE HAYDEN DUGGAN

AMS PRESS

NEW YORK

COLUMBIA UNIVERSITY
STUDIES IN THE
SOCIAL SCIENCES

39

The series was formerly known as
Studies in History, Economics and Public Law.

Reprinted with the permission of Columbia University Press
From the edition of 1902, New York
First AMS EDITION published 1970
Manufactured in the United States of America

Library of Congress Catalog Card Number: 76-120209
International Standard Book Number:
      Complete Set: 0-404-51000-0
      Number 39: 0-404-51039-6

AMS PRESS, INC.
New York, N.Y. 10003

810101

PREFACE

THE continued residence of the Ottoman Turks in Europe is due to two causes: the jealousy of the Christian powers, and the lack of unity among the subject Christian peoples of the Balkans. With the latter cause, this thesis is concerned only in so far as it is necessary to an understanding of the former. The first chapter, therefore, treats of the races of the Balkans, their attitude towards each other and their relations with foreign states. Though my subject is the diplomatic side of the Turkish question, the thesis is by no means a history of Turkey, nor even a diplomatic history of Turkey. It practically begins with the treaty of Kainardji, of 1774; for though the maintenance of the integrity of the Ottoman Empire was considered essential to the balance of power in Europe before then, the positions held by the various European states on the Turkish question, and especially by England and Russia, really date from that treaty.

The materials for this thesis have been taken from a number of sources. The collections of treaties have been carefully examined. Dumont's Corps Diplomatique, Wenck's Codex Juris Gentium, De Testa's collection of Ottoman treaties, De Clercq's of French, Neumann's of Austrian, and Martens' of Russian, not only give the texts of the treaties themselves, but also generally the notes, protocols and conventions associated with them. And the Histoire des Traités de Paix of De Garden and that of Schoell have frequently clarified what has been obscure in the collections. Much information was obtained from the Annual Register, and from Lesur's Annuaire Historique. Hertslet's Map of Europe by Treaty has been very helpful for the nineteenth century. The British and Foreign State Papers, the Parliamentary Papers and Hansard's Parliamentary Debates were invaluable. I have not had access to the French foreign papers, but Sorel's "Les Instructions données aux Ambassadeurs et Ministres de France" have been of much service. Many of the memoirs of statesmen, such as Metternich and Bismarck, and the lives of others, like Palmerston, the Prince Consort and Napoleon III., throw light on the motives which have actuated policies. With the exception of the first chapter, the matter of which was gathered principally from the works of others, the statements in this thesis have been made from the above sources. I have not hesitated to use the treatises of other men and sometimes have adopted their views, but in every case have made a foot-note to that effect. The works of two authors must be specially mentioned. Von Hammer's "Geschichte des Osmanischen Reiches" is the mine from which every writer on Turkey digs. Unfortunately, his great work ends with the Treaty of Kainardji, where this thesis practically begins. Debidour's "Histoire Diplomatique," though it begins at 1814, is a guide which I have freely consulted.

In conclusion, I gratefully acknowledge that the advice and encouragement given by Professor John Bassett Moore have been more valuable than the aid received from any books.

S. P. H. D.

COLLEGE OF THE CITY OF NEW YORK, *April 25, 1902.*

CONTENTS

PAGE

CHAPTER I

TURKS, RAYAHS AND FRANKS

The mixed character of the population of the Balkans—Turkish administration—The subject peoples—The Greeks—The Roumanians—The Servians and Bulgarians—The Montenegrins and Albanians—The relations of the Turks with the Franks—The Capitulations—The exclusive privileges of the French. .   11

CHAPTER II

THE TREATY OF KAINARDJI OF 1774

The decline of the Turks—The treaty of Carlowitz, 1699—The conflict with Peter the Great—The victories of Prince Eugene—Turkey and the European diplomacy of the eighteenth century—The treaty of Belgrade, 1739—Turkey and the Polish question—The struggle with Catherine II.   27

CHAPTER III

RUSSIAN AGGRESSION

Potemkin and the annexation of the Crimea—The designs of Catherine II. and Joseph II. on Turkey—The war of 1778–1792—The French invasion of Egypt—The revolt of the Servians—The war of 1806–1812—Turkey and the treaty of Tilsit—The treaty of Bucharest of 1812   47

CHAPTER IV

THE GREEK REVOLUTION

Turkey and the Congress of Vienna—Ali Pasha of Janina—The revolt of the Greeks—Nicholas I. becomes Emperor of Russia—The Russian demands granted—The treaty of London of July 1, 1827—The battle of Navarino—War with Russia—The treaty of Adrianople   61

CHAPTER V

THE EGYPTIAN REBELLION

Mehemet Ali, Pasha of Egypt—The treaty of Unkiar Skelessi of 1833—The rebellion of 1839—The attitude of the European Powers—The quadruple alliance of 1840—The excitement in France—The defeat of Mehemet Ali—The treaty of the Straits of 1841—The question of the Hungarian refugees . .   81

CHAPTER VI

THE CRIMEAN WAR

Quarrel between the Latin and Greek monks in the Holy Places—The plans of Nicholas—The mission of Mentschikoff—The Vienna note—Turkey declares war against Russia, Oct. 4, 1853—The massacre of Sinope—The position of Austria and Prussia—France and England declare war against Russia, March 27, 1854—The Austro-Prussian treaty of April 20, 1854—The four points—Sardinia joins the allies—Death of Nicholas I.—Fall of Sebastopol—The Congress of Paris of 1856—Terms of the treaty—Results of the Crimean war . .   99

CHAPTER VII

THE TREATY OF BERLIN

The decay and disintegration of the Ottoman Empire after 1856—The revolt of 1875 in Herzegovinia and in Bosnia—The Andrassy note—The Berlin memorandum—The Bulgarian atrocities—The conference of Constantinople—Russia delares war against Turkey, April 24, 1877—The fall of Plevna and the treaty of San Stefano—Excitement in England—The Cyprus convention—The Congress of Berlin—The terms of the treaty. 126

CHAPTER VIII

PRESENT STATUS OF THE EASTERN QUESTION

The union of Bulgaria and Eastern Roumelia, 1885—The Cretan and Armenian insurrections, 1889–1896—The Turco-Greek war of 1897—The English control of Egypt—Present attitude of the European Powers to Turkey. 147

CHAPTER I

TURKS, RAYAHS AND FRANKS

DURING the period of the Roman Empire the Balkan Peninsula was inhabited by three different races : Hellenes, the forefathers of the present Greeks ; Illyrians, the ancestors of the Albanians of to-day ; and the Thracians and Dacians, who, although geographically separate, were of the same race, and who became more Romanized than either of the other two, and adopted the Latin tongue. These last were the progenitors of the Roumanians (Romanians) of the present day, comprising the Wallachians (Vlachs) and Moldavians. The Wallachians, however, are not confined to the territory that bears their name, but are found scattered over Macedonia and Thessaly. During the sixth and seventh centuries there forced themselves among these races the various Slavonic tribes whose descendants, including the Servians, Bosnians, Herzegovinians, and Montenegrins, to-day inhabit the Balkans. Though many of the Greeks remained in the plains and valleys, they were for the most part driven to the coast, or to the large towns which the primitive methods of Slavonic warfare were unable to reduce. The Albanians were compelled to retire to the mountains of the western part of the peninsula, which they inhabit to this day. As the Slavonic invader came chiefly from the northwest, the Dacians, whose territory lay to the east on the Black Sea, remained comparatively unaffected. The newcomers and the old inhabitants never fused, as did the people of the Western Roman Empire, but established themselves side by side and maintained their separate nationalities, languages and customs. In the tenth century a Turanian tribe, the Bulgars,

coming from the northeast, pushed through the Dobrudja into
what is now Bulgaria and imposed their sway upon the Slavonic inhabitants; but in less than three centuries they became
thoroughly assimilated by the conquered and undistinguish-
able from them.   So that when the Ottoman conquest of the
Balkan peninsula occurred in the fourteenth and fifteenth
centuries, it was already peopled by Greeks, Albanians, Bulgarians, Servians, Bosnians, Herzegovinians and Montenegrins,
and the Roumanians, comprehending the Moldavians and
Wallachians.   In some parts of the peninsula each nation
formed the much greater portion of the inhabitants, but in
other districts, particularly in those which constitute the present Turkey in Europe, there was and is a medley of races,
each remaining distinct from the other, and each filled with
prejudice and animosity toward the remainder.   In the cities
there must be added to this admixture of peoples, Jews, Armenians, and the various European races by the Turks indiscriminately denominated as Franks.   Under any conditions, it would
be difficult to form a single stable state in the Balkans; the
conditions under which the Turks entered made it inevitable
that they should fail to do so.   Unlike the other invaders of
the Balkans they came not as heathen, unconnected with any
established form of worship, but as representatives of a great
religion which enjoined upon its adherents the duty of ex-
terminating or enslaving the unbeliever.   The Turks became
an army of occupation in a conquered country, and such they
have remained ever since.[1]

To the Turk, government consists in the maintenance of
his supremacy and the collection of tribute, and if these are
not resisted he is contemptuously tolerant of the usages of his
subjects.   After the conquest, therefore, the rayahs, the
Christian inhabitants, besides being allowed to retain a part of
their property, were permitted to exercise their religion on
conditions which would mark them off as an inferior part of

[1] Freeman, *Ottoman Power in Europe*, chap. ii.

the community.   Besides the land tax, which is a tithe paid by all the inhabitants of whatever religion, they paid the Kharadj or capitation tax, as a tribute for their unbelief.   The customs duty, levied alike on imports and exports, amounted to 2½ per cent. when the goods were Mohammedan, but to 5 per cent. when they belonged to an unbeliever.   The rayahs were also forbidden to carry arms or use horses, and their costumes were required to be of a nature to distinguish them from the true believer.   But the hardest of the Turkish impositions was the tribute of children.   Every fourth year Turkish officials appeared in the Christian villages and selected the strongest and most intelligent fifth of the children between the ages of six and nine, who were to become the slaves of the Sultan.   They were sent to Constantinople and educated as Moslems, and were taught that it was a privilege as well as a duty to assist in the propagation of the true faith.   A few of them entered the civil service, but the majority entered the corps of Janissaries.   This celebrated body consisted exclusively of those who had been tribute children.   They received regular pay, but were not allowed to marry nor to engage in any business.   Entirely cut off from their early Christian association, having a contempt for and being at enmity with the Timariot or Mohammedan feudal soldiery, they were at the absolute command of the Sultan; and until the decay of the Ottoman Empire they formed the best army in Europe. While the rayahs thus supplied their enemy with his finest weapon, they were themselves deprived of their most virile element, and we hear of no rebellious show of discontent with their condition until the system of tribute children fell into disuse two hundred years later.

As the Turk makes no distinction between church and state, the civil and the ecclesiastical law being founded on the Koran, it was natural for him to place the various subject peoples under the supervision of their spiritual heads.   The Greek and Armenian patriarchs and the Jewish chief rabbi, for example, were regarded by the Porte as the civil and religious heads of their respective nations and many administrative functions were performed by them; all law suits between members of their *millet*, *i. e.*, religious community, being in the last analysis settled by them. If the parties belonged to different *millets* and could not settle their difficulty by arbitration, the case went to the Turkish tribunals. After the decay of the Ottoman Empire began, in the seventeenth century, the corruption of the Turkish tribunals was equalled only by the rapacity of the tax gatherers.

Immediately after the conquest, the conquered territory was divided into provinces; but the Turks have always permitted local self-government. Over each province was placed a bey,[1] who was the head of the feudal soldiery of his pashalik. The people of each village elected their own elders, who assessed and collected the taxes which were demanded of the village, and the Kodja-Bashi, or headman, with the assistance of the parish priest, settled all disputes between the villagers unless they were of so important a nature as to be referred to the spiritual head.[2]

Before the decline, the government of the provinces was well administered, and the native population gained a great advantage in escaping from the petty tyranny of the local despots who had flourished under the weak Byzantine government.[3] But Turkish virility and honesty in administration disappeared after the reign of Suleiman the Great (1520–1566). The provincial pashas, especially those far removed from the central government, came thereafter to exercise almost absolute power. Besides, as they held office at the pleasure of the Sultan, their

---

[1] The title of pasha was originally one of mere honor, implying that the person was in the highest employ of the state. Gradually it became confined to leaders of forces, especially when they became governors of provinces.

[2] Urquhart, *Turkey and its Resources*. Chapters ii. and iii. give an excellent description of local self-government in Turkey.

[3] Finlay, *History of Greece*, vol. ii, p. 1.

tenure was uncertain; and as they usually obtained their appointment by the purchase of influence and favor at court, and as their salaries were nominal rather than real, they were obliged to resort to extortion and corruption in order to reimburse themselves. Moreover, their subordinates were appointed from Constantinople, often as spies, and these had to be conciliated. If a pasha, being exceptionally honest, tried to govern well and won the good will of his people, he was likely to be removed, since the Porte preferred an official who merely filled his pockets to one who might, by reason of his popularity, become dangerous. Provided the pasha sent to Constantinople the required revenue, the government cared little how he gathered it or how much more he gathered.[1] Of this vicious system, the rayahs, with no superior authority to appeal to, felt the full weight.

From the very beginning the Turkish government adopted the pernicious policy of farming the taxes. Until 1695, the grant was for one year only, and each tax-farmer wrung out of the people all he could during that year, lest he be outbid for the privilege in the next. It was a common thing for a tax-farmer, who had a rich district, to become opulent out of the proceeds of a single year. This system was not confined to one species of tax, but applied indiscriminately to all—customs, land, capitation and other forms. The farmer-general of a province often was the pasha, or some other high official, who sublet the various districts usually to Jews or Greeks. These farmers habitually employed as collectors soldiers, whose pay was generally months in arrears, but who yet had to live. Indeed, in the gathering of taxes, all agencies of the government, military as well as civil, were so united in interest that complaint by the sufferers was useless and practically impossible. Of all the immense sums extorted from the rayahs, and the almost equally unfortunate Turkish peasantry, only a small part reached the treasury; but the system was fast hurry-

[1] Odysseus, *Turkey in Europe*, p. 150 *et seq.*

ing the state to its ruin. The Hatti-sheriff of Gulhané (1839)[1] promulgated reforms, such as the separation of various functions formerly united in one person, and the prohibition of leases of taxes to officials, but without avail. The officials obtained contracts in the name of other persons, and then sublet them to rapacious usurers.[2]

The land of the conquered was divided into three kinds. One portion was set off for religious purposes, such as the building of mosques and schools, and this was called vakouf land. It paid no taxes, nor could it be confiscated or taken for civil purposes. The amount of this land was much increased by direct donations of the faithful, but even more by devices similar to those against which the mortmain laws were made in England. It was a common thing for the holder of unencumbered land to deed it to a mosque for a tenth of its value. In return, there was granted to him the right to lease it on payment of a rent equal to the interest on the money the mosque paid for it. During his lifetime, he could sell the lease, and at his death, his heirs inherited it. So extensively was this system practised, that by the middle of the last century, more two-thirds of the territory was vakouf. The consequent loss of revenue to the treasury gave rise to increased demands upon the rayahs.

The second division of land was mirié or domain land. A part of this consisted of the Sultan's private property, and land the income of which was devoted to the expenses of administration; but the major portion was granted to persons who held it on condition of rendering military service. These timars, as they were called, furnished the feudal levies of the Porte. In the beginning their estates were not hereditary, but they soon became so, and the timariot became the chief supporters of the provincial pashas in their defiance of the central authority. This kind of land was tilled by rayahs, who

---

[1] Hatti-sheriff is an irrevocable edict signed by the Sultan.

[2] Ubicini, *Letters on Turkey*, vol. i, letter 13.

suffered all the forms of oppression into which Turkish administration degenerated. The taxes were collected irregularly
and frequently, and the landlord was constantly devising fresh
methods of extortion.[1]

The third kind of land is mulk, or freehold land. The
amount of this in Turkey is not large, owing to the difficulty
of obtaining secure titles.[2]

Although the evils inseparable from Turkish administration
fell heavily upon the Christian rayahs, comparatively few of
them changed their faith. The Bosnian land owners, actuated
by the desire to save their property, and the small element of
Pomaks in Bulgaria, are instances to the contrary; but the
only case in which a large part of the population was converted was that of the semi-barbarous Albanians, whose Chris-
tianity was of a crude kind. The lot of the rayahs was not,
however, everywhere the same. In the large cities, where they
engaged in profitable trade, their burdens were comparatively
light. Especially was this the case in the capital, where the
taxes were not farmed, and where, in later times, the rayahs enjoyed to a great extent the good offices of the foreign ambassadors. It was in the provinces, where foreign influences were
not felt, and which were difficult of access, the roads being few
and poor, that the rayahs suffered most. Nor in the provinces were the fates of the different races the same. The Bulgarians suffered most, the Roumanians least.

In discussing the condition of the Greeks under Ottoman
sway, we must carefully distinguish those who dwelt in the
rural districts, both of modern Greece and of modern Turkey,
from the Greek clergy and the inhabitants of the great cities,
and particularly from the Phanariot aristocracy of Constanti-

---

[1] One of the Sultan Mahmoud's (1808–1829) reforms was to abolish this system, and to-day the holders of Mirié lands cannot sell, transfer or mortgage them
without a license from the authorities, nor make them Vakouf without a special
permit from the Sultan.

[2] *The People of Turkey*, by a Consul's Daughter, vol. i, chap. vii.

nople. The rural inhabitants experienced to the full extent
Turkish oppression, and their history from the fifteenth to the
nineteenth century is almost a blank.   But, as a result of the
conquest, the influence of the Greek church and the power of
the Greek clergy were much increased.   One of the causes of
the fall of Constantinople was the opposition of the Greek
clergy to the last emperor, who had allied himself with Rome,
hoping thereby to gain aid against the Turk.   The Greek
clergy hated the Pope more than they did the Sultan, and preferred the latter in Constantinople to the former.   Mohammed
the Second, the Conqueror, adopted as his deliberate policy
the encouragement of this feeling and determined to use the
hierarchy for his own purpose.   He placed all the orthodox
Catholics of the Empire under the control of the Greek patri-
ach of Constantinople, and conferred upon him the rank of
pasha.   Under the Byzantine emperors the patriarch had control over ecclesiastical affairs, but there was now delegated to
him supervision over a large number of civil matters.   All
questions of marriage, divorce and inheritance; all disputes
between Christians which did not concern Moslems in any
way, were committed to his charge or that of his subordinates.
He was granted the right of collecting tithes and dues, and of
enforcing his commands by excommunication, which few
orthodox Catholics dared incur.   In the course of time his
powers became as extensive in civil matters as in religious.
And the powers of the Greek metropolitans and bishops were
proportionately great.   The result of the introduction of this
system was to make these offices much sought after.   Simony
soon developed, and the patriarchate was sold to the highest
bidder, often bringing as much as one hundred thousand
ducats.   The patriarchs reimbursed themselves by charges
for consecrating bishops; the bishops by charges for consecrating priests; and these in turn by charges for performing
the simplest rites of the church for the people.   After the decline of the Ottoman Empire began, the Sultan frequently

deposed the patriarch in order to put the place up for sale again, and the clergy did not scruple to buy the influence of officials and of women of the harem in the scramble for the post. In return for the privileges they enjoyed, the clergy became the willing instruments of Turkish tyranny, enjoining obedience to the government, smothering nationalistic movements, excommunicating leaders. Their rapacity and avarice equalled that of the Turkish governors, and the people heard with as much dread of the visit of the Greek bishop to their district as of the presence of the Turkish pasha. Amid this carnival of venality and corruption, indulged in by monks and the higher clergy of the Greek orthodox church, the married parish priests of the rural districts remained comparatively pure. They were bigoted and fanatical, but they shared the burdens of their flocks and kept them true to the faith and to the nation.[1]

The Turk is no money-getter; and the control of commerce and finance soon fell almost entirely into the hands of the Greeks, though in recent times they share it with Jews and Armenians. It was not remarkable, therefore, that the Greek merchant families of the Phanor[2] acquired in course of time great wealth, with which they could buy privileges from the Turk; and a Greek aristocracy rose at Constantinople which played for a century and a half a most prominent part in the affairs of the Ottoman Empire. It is a peculiar anomaly that although the Turks have ruled the Balkans for over four hundred years, they have never had sufficient political or administrative ability to man the state with the necessary officials. For the first century and a half the tribute children supplied them with civil officials, as well as filled their armies. After the decay of that system, Christian renegades furnished the necessary material, the majority of the grand viziers

[1] Finlay, *History of Greece.* For a vivid description of the condition of the Orthodox Church, see vol. v, chap. iii.

[2] The district of Constantinople inhabited by the patriarch and wealthy Greeks.

being of that class. But from the middle of the seventeenth
century, the high official class of Constantinople was recruited
almost entirely from the Phanariots. With the decline of
their military strength, the Turks found it necessary to have
more intimate and more constant relations with foreign powers,
but as they refused to learn either foreign languages or foreign
ways they fell to employing the Phanariots, who were adroit,
skillful and sufficiently servile. At first the latter occupied
only the humbler positions, such as interpreters and go-
betweens; but from the time of the greatest of Turkish grand
viziers, Kuprili Mohammed (1585–1661), almost the entire
control of foreign affairs and to a great extent of domestic
affairs fell into their hands. Kuprili Mohammed appointed
the Phanariot Panayoti as dragoman of the Porte, a position
which soon became analogous to that of minister. So successfully did this office work, that soon afterwards the position
of dragoman of the fleet was created. This official was
assistant to the Capudan Pasha or High Admiral, who not
only controlled the navy, but practically governed the Archipelago. The dragoman of the fleet soon obtained almost
complete power in the Aegean, buying from the Capudan
Pasha all the offices in his gift and then selling them at a
profit. It is hardly an exaggeration to say that at the beginning of the nineteenth century the Balkans were governed
as much by Greeks as by Turks. The influence of the
Phanariot aristocracy, as well as that of the Constantinople
patriarchate, was broken by the Greek Revolution. Both had
in the beginning opposed the movement as destructive to their
selfish interests and their influence; and after the revolution
the Porte became suspicious of Christian officials, while one
of the first desires of the new Greek state was the establishment of a national church.

What is now Roumania was not in the path of the warfare
which the Turks constantly waged with Hungary and Venice.
It never became a province of the Turkish Empire, nor was it

much influenced by the Turks. On the contrary, in the early part of the sixteenth century, an agreement was made between the two principalities of which it is now composed and the Porte, by which the former were to become a vassal state of Turkey and pay an annual tribute, but were to have the exclusive management of their own affairs. No Turks were to be admitted into the two principalities, and they were freely to elect their hospodars or governors.[1] The Roumanians are the only people of the Balkans who have an aristocracy of birth, Turkish dislike to hereditary rank having destroyed it among the Greeks and Slavs. The Roumanian Boyards, however, could not brook the rule of any one of their own families, and in the contest for the office of hospodar some of them did not hesitate to invoke Turkish influence and favor. The result was that in time the Porte appointed and maintained the hospodars, usually giving the office to the highest bidder among the Boyards. This system ended in 1711. In the war of that year with Peter the Great, the hospodars were found aiding the Russians; and from that time until 1821, the beginning of the Greek Revolution, they were appointed directly by the Sultan, and although never Mohammedans, were usually Phanariot Greeks. They bought their privileges from the Porte, and they exercised their powers of office chiefly for the ends of personal gain, and of filling all offices in church and state with their own class. After the Greek Revolution, the Porte appointed natives to the position, and a national party arose antagonistic to both Greek and Turk, which succeeded finally, as we shall see, in working out independence for the country.

The lot of the Slavonic inhabitants of the Ottoman Empire was for four hundred years indeed pitiable. The Servians to a great extent, and the Bulgarians entirely, disappeared from history. Bulgaria, lying helpless and hopeless immediately behind Adrianople, the first capital of the Turks, from the

[1] De Testa, *Recueil des Traités de la Porte Ottomane*, vol. v, p. 283.

beginning resigned itself to oblivion and oppression. The Servians, farthest removed from the central government, which could not control the local officials, were for a large part of the period a prey to the organized brigandage of Janissary rebels.[1] The national churches of both nations were destroyed; and as a reward for their fidelity to the Christian faith they suffered four centuries of a twofold tyranny, that of Turkish pashas and Greek priests. The Phanariot clergy sent from Constantinople wrung from the people as much money as possible for Hellenic schools and institutions at Constantinople, if not for more questionable purposes. The native Slavonic priests, who were poor and ignorant, possessed little influence among the people, whom the Phanariots endeavored in every way to Hellenize. Educated Bulgarians until within almost a generation called themselves Greeks; and we shall see with what difficulty those nations recovered their lost independence and their national churches. Only the Montenegrins and Albanians, of the Christian population in the Balkans, were able to maintain themselves against Turk and Phanariot. The Montenegrins were never conquered, and the Albanians, in their mountain fortresses, proved so difficult and costly to subdue that the Turks were glad to make terms with them, granting practical independence.

The Koran, which in Turkey is the source of all law, civil and ecclesiastical, divides the earth into two parts: Dar-ul-Islam, i. e., the house of Islam, and Dar-ul-Harb, the house of the enemy. The only relation the former can have with the latter is the Djihad, or Holy War. Such a relation, so long as its existence was active, prevented the maintenance of any international law between Turks and Franks, and their intercourse was determined entirely by exigencies. Indeed it was not until 1856 that by the treaty of Paris the Ottoman Empire was formally admitted to the benefits of the European system. But the necessities of commerce and afterwards military weak-

[1] Ranke, *History of Servia*, chap. iii.

ness constrained the Turks to enter into peaceful international
relations with the Christian states of Europe; and until 1856
the international law governing their relations with foreign
states was founded on treaties called capitulations, which to a
great extent embodied the previous customary laws with regard to Franks. The capitulations are actual treaties; but,
according to the Sheri or ecclesiastical law, only truces, not
treaties, could be made with infidels. Besides, according to
Mohammedan ideas, the Sultan was the Lord of the world,
having no equal with whom he could conclude a treaty. The
international instruments, by which privileges were granted to
the inferior infidel nations, without requiring any reciprocal
obligations, were therefore called capitulations, and from them
has arisen that peculiar condition of things by which the residents of foreign nationality form separate communities within
the Turkish dominions.

The Franks, or Christian foreigners, are divided into two
classes: (1) Those possessing official privileges, viz., ministers
and consuls, and (2) the ordinary private individuals. A consul in the Turkish dominions practically enjoys the privileges
which in the case of an ambassador are comprehended under
the term exterritoriality. His person and house are inviolable;
he is not subject to the local law, civil or criminal; he pays no
personal taxes or custom duties, and his privileges extend to
his family and suite. But he also has powers which do not
ordinarily belong to an ambassador. He exercises civil and
to some extent criminal jurisdiction over his fellow countrymen. It is his duty to preserve law and order in the community of which he is the judicial and administrative head; in
a word, the consulate is the seat of government on a small
scale for all persons under its flag.

To a great extent, an ordinary foreigner in the Levant also
enjoys the privileges of exterritoriality. He is subject in civil
and, to a great extent, in criminal matters only to the jurisdiction of his consul. His legal domicil is in his own country

His house is inviolable, no Turkish official being permitted to enter it except with the consul's permission. His real property, however, is subject to the law of the land. If he engages in litigation with a foreigner of a different nationality, the case is decided not in the local tribunals, but in the consular court of the defendant. These are extensive privileges and they sometimes give rise to conflict with the local authorities, especially as they are much envied by the native rayahs, who attempt at times to take advantage of them.[1]

Although the Porte granted capitulations to the Genoese, Venetians and Pisans before 1535, the French capitulations of that year were more important, because of the greater extent of the privileges which they conferred and because they served as a model for those afterwards granted to other countries.[2] Moreover, in European history, they mark the beginning of that great influence which France has since almost continuously enjoyed, an influence unequaled by that of any other nation. The capitulations of 1535 confirmed the powers of the foreign consuls and the privileges of foreign residents; but a great extension of privileges to France was granted by the capitulations of 1604 and by later ones. There was granted to her citizens freedom of worship; the Holy Places in Palestine were to be safeguarded by her religious functionaries, who were not to be disturbed; Frankish priests and dependents, of whatever nation, were not to be annoyed in the exercise of their functions. These privileges were so construed by the French as to include the right of protection of all Catholics in the East.[3]

---

[1] Van Dyck, *Ottoman Capitulations.* An excellent account of the origin, development, and present status of the Turkish capitulations.

[2] De Testa, *Recueil des Traités de la Porte Ottomane,* vol. i, p. 15; Charrière, *Négotiations de la France dans le Levant,* vol. i, p. 285; Flassan, *Diplomatie Française,* vol. i, p. 366.

[3] It is curious that so many of the English writers on the Eastern Question refer the privilege obtained by France to safeguard the Holy Places to the capitulations

The commercial privileges granted were also large. French ships secured freedom of traffic in all Ottoman seas, the navigation of which was also forbidden to the ships of other states with which the Porte had no friendly treaties, unless they sailed under the French flag. As Venice was the only other state that had a commercial treaty with the Porte in the sixteenth century, the advantage thus obtained by France in the East is obvious. Her flag was seen everywhere in the Levant, on the shipping in the harbors, on the monasteries in the interior; pilgrims journeyed under her protection to the Holy Places, and her ambassador was ever ready to maintain the rights of the Giaour at the capital. The French capitulations were frequently violated but were always renewed, and in 1740 all the special privileges granted to France were solemnly confirmed; and we shall see that it was a violation of these privileges in the nineteenth century that was the occasion, if not the cause, of the French participation in the Crimean War.

The capitulations of 1535 were inspired by mutual considerations of expediency and policy. The power of the House of Hapsburg in Spain, Germany, Italy and the Netherlands menaced the very existence of France. The House of Hapsburg was also the chief enemy of the Ottoman Empire; and the object of the French alliance with the Mohammedan Turk for more than two hundred years was the abasement of the House of Austria. It was to France that the Porte almost invariably turned for advice when in trouble, and the friendship between the two countries was constant, though severely strained by Louis XIV and Napoleon I. It is worthy of note that in a short time the relations between the Porte and

of 1535. There is not a word in them about those places. Nor does the firman of 1528, wherein Solyman granted to the French in Egypt the privileges enjoyed there before its conquest by the Ottomans, contain any reference to the Holy Places. The first mention of them that I can find is in the capitulations of 1604. The source of the error is probably D'Ohsson, *Tableau Général de l'Empire Ottomane.*

France became so cordial that the King of France, Henry IV, was referred to in 1604 as Padishah, *i. e.*, Great Ruler or Emperor. This title was reserved by the Moslems for the Sultan as being without equal on earth, and it was with extreme reluctance in the nineteenth century that they gradually extended it to some of the other rulers of the great states of Europe.

Until the latter part of the eighteenth century the Porte never maintained permanent embassies at the various European capitals, although other states had such embassies at Constantinople. The Ottoman capital indeed was not a desirable post, for the foreign ambassador was often treated with contempt and insult, and even thrown into the prison of the Seven Towers, especially on the outbreak of a war between his country and Turkey. The conduct of negotiations with the Porte required great skill in diplomacy and even greater skill in the effective use of money. In the nineteenth century, however, a great change took place in the diplomatic intercourse between the Porte and other powers.

CHAPTER II

THE TREATY OF KAINARDJI

THE power of the Turks reached its zenith in the reign of Solyman the Great (1520–1566), and except for intermittent revivals of energy, the decline after his death was steady. He was the last of the great Sultans who personally conducted the government and led the armies in the field. After him the administration of government fell into the hands of the grand viziers, and the Sultans devoted themselves chiefly to the pleasures of the harem. With the completion of the conquest, habits of luxury became general among the official class, and the old martial spirit decayed. While the Turk was thus declining in power, his Christian enemies were growing stronger. In the seventeenth century feudalism in Europe began to decay, succumbing to the development of the national state. Monarchs ceased to rely on feudal levies and maintained armies of trained soldiers, furnished with the new weapons of warfare. The Turk, on the other hand, lost his old discipline and refused to adopt that of Europe. The greatest blow to his military power was the revolution in the constitution of the Janissaries. At first they were permitted to marry, then to introduce their children into the corps. and finally to allow Turks to serve in it. Thus the institution of the tribute children gradually died out, the last instance of its enforcement being in 1676. The Christian rayahs were no longer depleted of their best and strongest, while the Porte lost its most efficient weapon. With the great depreciation of the currency, which took place in the seventeenth and eighteenth centuries, came a corresponding fall in the wages

of the Janissaries, who were soon allowed to enter trades and
to supply substitutes for foreign service. They remained
chiefly at Constantinople, the most turbulent part of the
population, opposed to all reform, fomenting rebellion, more
dangerous to the Turkish than to any other government. It
was a fortunate thing for the Ottoman Empire that the Christian states devoted themselves during the first half of the
seventeenth century to their religious wars, and did not unite
against the common enemy.

The diplomacy of continental Europe during the latter half
of the seventeenth century and the former half of the eighteenth was determined by the rivalry of the Houses of Haps-
burg and Bourbon. Finding herself endangered by the union
of Spain and Austria, France erected what has been known in
French diplomacy as the Barrier of the East, *i. e.*, the union of
Sweden, Poland and Turkey with France against the house of
Austria. Until the reign of Peter the Great, the Barrier of the
East proved very efficacious, France usually being able to
obtain the support of one of her allies in her contests with
Austria. But with the growth of Russia came a change.
Russia, desirous of expanding to the south and west,
naturally came into conflict with the Barrier, and as naturally
allied herself with the enemy of the Barrier, Austria, at first
tacitly, and then by the formal compact of August 6, 1726.[1]
This situation continued with but few changes until what is
known in diplomatic history as the Overthrow of the Alliances
in 1756, caused by the rise of Prussia. Austria, finding she
had more to fear from Prussia than from France, and France,
conceiving that her chief enemy was not Austria but England,
renounced their hereditary enmity in 1756 and became allies.[2]
France by no means broke with her allies of the Barrier, viz.,
Sweden, Poland and Turkey. On the contrary she supported
them uniformly; but as their existence was no longer indis-

[1] Dumont, *Corps Diplomatique*, vol. vii, part 2, p. 131.

[2] Wenck, *Codex Juris Gentium*, vol. iii, p. 141.

pensable against Austria, she supported them to maintain the
equilibrium of the East. As a counterpoise to the union of
the houses of Hapsburg and Bourbon, Catherine II. formed
the System of the North, founded on an alliance between
Russia, Prussia and England. The System of the North
lasted until the American Revolution, when the exorbitant
pretensions of Prussia, especially in Poland, and the abuse of
power by England on the seas caused Catherine to approach
first Austria and then France; and when the French Revolution broke out, a plan of a quadruple alliance of Russia,
Austria, France and Spain against Great Britain and Prussia
was under discussion.[1] We must now trace the influence of
these diplomatic changes on the fortunes of Turkey.

The bigotry of the Hapsburg emperor, Leopold I, caused
the Hungarian rebellion of 1682. The grand vizier of the Ottoman Empire at that time was Kara Mustapha, who owed his
office to the circumstance that he was son-in-law to the Sultan,
and in whom wild ambitions were united with mean abilities.
He sought to take advantage of the Hungarian rebellion, not
only to conquer that part of Hungary which still remained to
the House of Austria, but to set up a Turkish pashalik of his
own at Vienna.[2] His army, however, was utterly defeated
before Vienna by John Sobieski, King of Poland, who had
come to the rescue of Austria, and the result of the defeat was
the immediate declaration of war against Turkey by Russia
and Venice. For seventeen years the Turks attempted to defend themselves against these combined attacks, but each year
saw their frontiers receding towards Constantinople. Once
more the quarrels of the Christian states saved the Ottoman
Porte. Louis XIV, who had aided the Hungarian rebels and
had inspired the Ottoman policy, was exhausted by his struggle

---

[1] For a complete view of the diplomacy of the seventeenth and eighteenth centuries, see "*Recueil des Instructions données aux Ambassadeurs et Ministres de
France*," especially the volumes relating to Russia and Austria.

[2] Von Hammer, *Geschichte des Osmanischen Reiches*, book 48.

against half of Europe, and was compelled to sign the treaty
of Ryswick in 1697. This would have enabled the Austrians
to turn their entire forces against the Turks, had the general
European situation permitted it. William III., of England,
the soul of the alliance against Louis XIV., endeavored to
bring about peace between Austria and the Porte. He foresaw the inevitable struggle over the Spanish succession, and
wished the entire strength of Austria to be exerted against
France. Lord Paget, the English ambassador at Constantinople, offered the mediation of England to the Porte, and at
the instance of William he was seconded by the Dutch ambassador. Louis used strenuous efforts to prevent the Porte
from making peace, assuring it that the peace of Ryswick was
but a temporary truce, and exhorting it to continue the
struggle until France should be ready for war. But Louis'
reverses had, for the moment, impaired French prestige at
Constantinople, where English influence now stood high, and
the Porte listened to the suggestions of England. Negotiations were opened at Carlowitz, on the Danube, on the basis
of the Uti Possidetis, *i. e.*, that each power should keep the
territory which was in its possession at the beginning of negotiations. The Porte protested against this, as it would involve
the loss of some of its finest territories, but Austria insisted, and
the Porte had to give way. All the contestants were anxious
for peace except Peter the Great, whose armies had conquered
Azof, and who hoped to gain still more by continuing the war.
He entreated the Emperor to keep up the struggle, warning
him that England and Holland were actuated by selfish considerations. His entreaties, however, were in vain ; and although certain deviations were made from the Uti Possidetis,
the treaty of Carlowitz [1] was signed January 26, 1699, on that
basis. The Ottoman Empire lost many of its fairest provinces.
Austria obtained practically all of Hungary and Transyl-
vania ; Poland secured Podalia and the Ukraine ; Venice, the

---

[1] Dumont, *Corps Diplomatique*, vol. vii, part 2, p. 448.

Morea ; Russia, Azof. Moreover, all payments of tribute by the Christian powers to the Porte were abolished. But it is not the loss of territory, however great, which makes the treaty of Carlowitz so important in European history, but the change in the relative positions of the parties. The Ottoman Empire, till then so dreaded by Christendom, lost its military prestige, sank into a position almost devoid of diplomatic influence, and became a political machine which could be used by the European powers in future to serve their own selfish ends.[1] Austria, menaced so long on the south, found herself consolidated and with a splendid military frontier. And for the first time Russia obtained a foothold near the Black Sea.

Peter the Great was determined that his dominions should reach the sea both on the west and the south, but to accomplish this purpose he must come into conflict with Sweden and Turkey. Both these countries feared the growth of the Muscovite power, and in the diplomacy of the eighteenth century we find Sweden and Turkey working together. In his contest with the Swedes, Peter was eventually successful, and after Pultowa (1709) the Swedish king, Charles XII., found refuge in Turkish territory. A diplomatic struggle then began in Constantinople. From the outbreak of the war of the Spanish Succession, Feriol, the French ambassador, had been urging the Porte to retrieve its fortunes by declaring war against its former enemies in conjunction with France. He was now strongly seconded by Poniatowsky, Charles XII.'s agent at Constantinople. Sutton and Collyer, the English and Dutch ambassadors, were for a number of years able by persuasion and by bribery, to which all ambassadors at Constantinople resorted, to prevent hostile action by the Porte. The Turks were not desirous of war, but they watched with grave anxiety the growth of the Russian fleet in the Sea of Azof, and the erection of strong fortresses on the Russian southern border. Moreover, the frequent violations of Turkish territory by

---

[1] Schlosser, *History of the Eighteenth Century*, vol. iii, introduction.

the Russians caused the greatest indignation at Constantinople, and this feeling, inflamed by French and Swedish intrigues, led the Porte finally to declare war against Russia November 28, 1710. Peter was taken at a disadvantage, being at war with the Swedes in the north, but he led an army in person towards the Danube. The Russians in this war adopted the practice, which was to become so prominent a part of their policy with reference to Turkey, of rousing the subject Christian peoples, and an agreement was made with Cantemir, hospodar of Moldavia, whereby he should rise in favor of Peter on the approach of the Russian army. In return Moldavia was to be made an independent state under Russian protection, the sovereignty to remain with Cantemir and his heirs.[1] Peter greatly relied on the assistance which he was to receive from the Moldavians, but his expectations were disappointed; and in June, 1711, he was surrounded by the Turkish army and compelled to agree to the humiliating Peace of the Pruth.[2] By this treaty Peter was obliged to give up all he had gained by the former war, to demolish his fortresses, to engage to abstain from interference in the affairs of Poland, and to forego the privilege of keeping an ambassador at Constantinople. To retrieve the disgrace of the Peace of the Pruth became for the next century one of the chief ends of Russian diplomacy.

Nothing in the treaty of Carlowitz so hurt the pride of the Turks as the cession of the Morea to feeble Venice, and the Porte waited for a favorable opportunity to retake it. That opportunity apparently presented itself in 1714, for although the war of the Spanish Succession was then ended, great discord prevailed among the states of Europe. The western powers were apprehensive of further trouble from Spain, and Peter was involved in war with the Swedes. Repeated collisions between Turkish and Venetian galleys furnished the Porte

[1] Schuyler, *Peter the Great*, vol. ii, chap. lxiii.

[2] Dumont, *Corps Diplomatique*, vol. viii, part 1, p. 275.

with a pretext, and by the end of 1715 the Turks had recon-
quered the whole of the Morea. Their rapid success alarmed
Austria. Moreover, the influence of Prince Eugene was then
paramount at Vienna, and he maintained that a war with the
Turks would not only afford an opportunity for territorial
aggrandizement, but would enable the army to be kept intact
without arousing the suspicions of the other Christian powers;
and it was deemed necessary to keep the army in a state of
readiness, as it was suspected that Alberoni would attempt to
recover the possessions lost by Spain to Austria by the Treaty
of Utrecht.[1] For these reasons the Emperor, Charles VI.,
decided to aid the Venetians, and on April 13, 1716, formed
with them an offensive and defensive alliance. Prince Eugene
was everywhere successful against the Turks, ending the war
by the capture of Belgrade. He would fain have followed up
these successes, but news arrived that Alberoni had landed
his Spaniards in Sardinia, and that another European war was
imminent. England and Holland again offered their mediation, and negotiations were opened at Passarowitz on the
Danube, July, 1718, on the basis of the Uti Possidetis. The
treaty of Passarowitz[2] was the most glorious ever signed by
Austria with Turkey. Not only did the Turks lose the Banat
of Temesvar, their last possession in Hungary, but they were
forced to surrender to Austria Little Wallachia, and Belgrade
and other important towns in Servia. The Turk was forever
removed from Hungary, which had hitherto been the cause of
most of the wars between Austria and Turkey. The Porte
had always found it easy to incite revolt against the Emperor
among the Hungarians, and the latter often preferred
the comparatively lenient rule of the Porte to the bigoted
tyranny of many of the Hapsburgs. Austria followed her
usual policy of caring only for her own territorial interests,
and left Venice, for whom she had professedly entered into the

[1] Schlosser, *History of the Eighteenth Century*, vol. iii, pages 250 *et seq.*

[2] De Testa, *Recueil des Traités de la Porte Ottomane*, vol. ix, p. 73.

war, to her fate. The Porte had no longer to fear Venice or Poland; in the eighteenth century its wars were carried on against Austria and Russia; in the nineteenth against Russia alone.

During the eighteenth century, three European states were in danger of dismemberment, viz., Sweden, Poland and Turkey. After the death of Charles XII., in 1718, the oligarchic party succeeded in gaining control of the government in Sweden,[1] and for fifty years the resulting dissensions left Sweden enfeebled and a prey to her neighbors. The oligarchic party was supported by Prussia and Russia, especially under Frederick the Great and Catherine II., for the same reason that they upheld the anarchic constitution of Poland; and it was under the oligarchic regime that Sweden lost all her Baltic possessions except Finland to Russia, and to Prussia most of her German possessions. The anarchic condition in which the Polish nobility consented to keep their country, by maintaining its oligarchic institutions, its elective kingship and its liberum veto,[2] made Poland an easy prey to her covetous neighbors, particularly Frederick and Catherine, who, with a view to the ultimate dismemberment of the country, obtained by treaty with the Poles the right to intervene to maintain their ruinous constitution.[3] That Turkey was enabled to survive the eighteenth century, was probably due to the fact that the attention of her ill-wishers was so constantly diverted to Sweden and Poland, and to the jealousy of Austria and Russia over the possession of the Danubian provinces.

The attitudes of the various European states towards the threatened countries were interesting. France, as stated above,

---

[1] Dumont, supplement 2, part 2, p. 149. "Convocation des Etats du Royaume de Suede par la reine Ulrique Eleonore avec declaration expresse qu'elle renonce au pouvoir absolu, communement nommé la souveraineté," December 26th, 1718.

[2] The right of an individual member of the Diet to prevent legislation by his single vote.

[3] Wenck, *Codex Juris Gentium*, vol. iii, p. 486, article secrét.

supported all three.   Since the capitulations of 1535, she had
been the ally of the Ottoman Porte, and her influence was
thrown constantly in favor of Turkey as against her enemies.
During the greater part of the eighteenth century, the Swedish
court was in the pay of the French.   And French statesmen
always believed the preservation of Poland to be necessary to
the balance of power in the East.   The attitude of England
towards the three states was dictated by her opposition to
France and her commercial interests.   The dismemberment of
Poland would affect those interests little, but would please
Russia, whereas the dismemberment of the other two states
would injure English interests considerably.   So that, although
England was friendly to Russia during the eighteenth century,
even at one time (1742) having a treaty of alliance with her,[1]
her influence was thrown at times in favor of Sweden; and
neither England nor Holland wished to lose so good a cus-
tomer as the Turk, or to see a Russian commerce grow up in
the Levant.   The course of Austria and Prussia was governed
entirely by the desire for territorial aggrandizement.   Prussia,
especially under Frederick the Great, was bent upon extending
her boundaries in whatever way and at whatsoever cost might
be necessary, and she gained her object by war and contriv-
ance and at the expense of Austria, Poland and Sweden.   Not
being able to profit by the dismemberment of Turkey, Frederick was interested in her fate only to the extent of using her
to create dissension between Russia and Austria.   Austria
profited largely by the Polish dismemberment, and she also
regarded the Turkish dominions as a legitimate field of exploi-
tation, but grew cautious and anxious when Russia became
her competitor.   The three threatened states, perceiving
their danger, saw the need of co-operation against their common enemy—Russia.   A treaty of alliance was, therefore, made
between Turkey and Sweden in 1739.[2]   It was a war with

[1] Wenck, *Codex Juris Gentium*, vol. i, p. 645.

[2] *Ibid.*, vol. i, p. 504.

Sweden which prevented Russia from taking part against Turkey in the conflict which ended at Passarowitz. It was a war
with Turkey which prevented Russia from interfering in Sweden, as Catherine wished to do in 1772, when Gustavus III.
overthrew the oligarchy and once more restored Sweden to
strength.[1] Poland might have allied herself with Turkey in
the eighteenth century, but for Russian domination. The
diplomacy of the eighteenth century was undoubtedly selfish
and corrupt, but it was the diplomacy of the eighteenth century
which prevented the dismemberment of Turkey.

The decade after the Treaty of Passarowitz saw Russia at
war with both Sweden and Poland, and she was successful
against both. In 1733 she found herself at peace with her
enemies, but with a splendid army of veterans under an able
commander, Marshal Münnich, and the time was deemed ex-
pedient to retrieve the disgrace of the Peace of the Pruth.
Moreover, the Turks had greatly weakened themselves in a
war with Persia, and besides had given offense to Russia by
calling her attention to that provision of the Peace of the
Pruth by which she had agreed not to interfere in Poland.
An excuse was easily found for beginning hostilities, since the
Turks never were able to restrain the Tartars of the Crimea
and Kuban from committing depredations. The Russians
began the war without a declaration. Marshal Münnich was
altogether successful, and the Turks were driven to accept
the proffered mediation of Austria, with whom by the Peace
of Passarowitz they were bound to maintain a twenty-five
years' truce. But by the Treaty of Vienna of 1726,[2] between
Austria and Russia, it was agreed that each power should
help the other with thirty thousand men in case either should
be at war with a third power. Russia now demanded the fulfilment of this engagement. The Austrian government long
debated whether it should merely fulfil the terms of the treaty,

[1] Rambaud, *Histoire de la Russie*, chap. xxx.

[2] Dumont, vol. viii, part 2, p. 131.

or take advantage of the situation of the Turks to make war
upon them and seize their territory. The war party prevailed, and a new treaty of alliance was made with Russia in
January, 1737, whereby the two states agreed to carry on the
war according to a stipulated plan and not to make peace
separately.[1]   During these negotiations, Austria kept up the
pretense of mediation between Russia and Turkey at the conference of Nimiroff, and used the time thus gained to put her
army in readiness.   Finally, Austria notified the Turks that
she would require as the price of peace the cession of Moldavia
and Wallachia.[2]   The conference then came to an end and
hostilities were renewed.   But the conditions under which
Austria went to war in 1737 were very different from those of
1716.   She no longer had a Prince Eugene to command her
armies.   The Emperor, Charles VI, was infirm and was a
victim of intrigues ; the finances were deplorably confused ;
the army was in a wretched condition, and the council was
divided.   The result was that the Austrians were everywhere
defeated ; and the Emperor requested Villeneuve, the French
Ambassador at Constantinople, to open negotiations for peace.[3]
French diplomacy was never more skillful than in the months
preceding the signing of the Treaty of Belgrade.   It roused
Sweden to preparations for war against Russia, and caused the
Poles to renew their struggle, thereby compelling Russia to
come to terms with the Turks.   Villeneuve used his position
as mediator, to which he had been appointed by Anne of
Russia, as well as by the Emperor, to sow dissensions between
the allies, to magnify the preparations and strength of the

---

[1] Martens, *Recueil des Traités conclus par la Russie*, vol. i, p. 69.

[2] Flassan, *Diplomatie Française*, vol. v, p. 102.

[3] The Austrians showed an intense avidity for peace. Charles VI. was very
infirm and might die at any time, and Maria Theresa and her husband were anxious to have the war off their hands in case of his demise. The generals in the
field, Wallis and Neipperg, who hated each other and were both incompetent,
showed an equally great desire to end the war.

Turks, and finally, to obtain for the latter a most favorable peace. By the treaty of Belgrade, September 12, 1739,[1] Austria relinquished nearly all her acquisitions made during the previous war, Little Wallachia and the places, including Belgrade, which she had obtained in Servia and in Bosnia. The Russians gained nothing by their great victories, except a slight increase of territory in the Ukraine, the basis of their settlement being practically the status quo ante bellum.

Though French influence was never so high at Constantinople as after 1740, the Ottoman Porte could not be tempted to engage in the war of the Austrian Succession. At the outbreak of the war France urged the Porte to join the allies in the spoliation of the Austrian dominions, but the Sultan refused to do so and offered his mediation to the Christian powers. Similarly, during the Seven Years' War, Turkey remained at peace externally, although the rapacity of the provincial pashas and the laxness which everywhere prevailed were preparing the way for the great fall which was soon to take place. In 1762 the greatest enemy that the Porte has ever known, Catherine II., ascended the Russian throne, and the next year there occurred an event which was specially fraught with misfortune to Turkey, viz., the death of Augustus III. of Saxony, King of Poland, which gave rise to the struggle for the Polish succession.

Immediately on the demise of Augustus III. France put forward another Saxon prince as her candidate for the Polish throne, and Austria, whose traditional attitude toward France had been reversed by Kaunitz by the treaty of 1756, gave him her support. Catherine put forth Stanislaus Poniatowski, one of her old lovers, and she was supported by Frederick the Great. Under the auspices of the Russian army the Polish diet elected Stanislaus, but he was able to retain his throne only by the aid of Russian bayonets, the Polish Confederates, as

[1] Wenck, *Codex Juris Gentium*, vol. i, p. 326. See also the French guarantee in De Testa's *Recueil des Traités de la Porte Ottomane*, vol. i, pp. 178 *et seq.*

those who opposed Russian intervention were called, having
taken up arms against him.   France dared not openly support
her candidate, as she had just emerged from the humiliating
Seven Years' War and was menaced by the attitude of England, who favored Russia.   But Choiseul, the French minister,
while giving secret assistance to the Confederates, began the
series of intrigues at Constantinople which finally terminated
in the war of 1768–1774, so full of disaster to Turkey.   The
able ambassador of France at Constantinople at this time was
the Count de Vergennes.   He did not hesitate to lay before
the court of Versailles the wretchedly disorganized condition
of Turkey ;[1] but Choiseul, bent on a diversion in favor of the
Poles, instructed Vergennes to redouble his efforts, to assure
the Porte of the neutrality of Austria, and to send to the
Crimea Baron de la Totte, who had much influence with the
Tartars there.   The peace party, however, was in power at
Constantinople, and had the Russians acted prudently war
might have been averted.   The Confederate Poles, when defeated on their own territory, took refuge in Turkey, and after
the manner of the Tartars made predatory excursions there-
from.   The Russians retaliated ; and when General Weissman
pursued the Poles across the Turkish border and laid the town
of Balta in ashes, the indignation of the Turks became violent
and the Sheikh-ul-Islam granted the necessary Fetva to commence war.[2]   But the Turks were wholly unprepared, without
money, artillery, fortifications or discipline, and the six weeks
which elapsed before they actively began hostilities were used

[1] Memoire de M. de Vergennes sur la Porte Ottomane, *Segur's Politique*, vol.
iii, pp. 115–142 *passim*.

[2] The Sheikh ul-Islam, or Mufti, is the head of the Ulema, a body both religious
and judicial, learned in the law, which is at the same time civil and ecclesiastical.
No decree emanating from the sovereign is valid without the Fetva, a kind of Bull
of the Mufti.   This was once formidable, but has become a mere judicial formal-
ity.   Schlosser, *History of Europe in the Eighteenth Century*, vol. iv, p. 404,
says: "The delay in granting the Fetva in this case was the result of the inferior
size of Russian as against French bribes."

by the Russians in reducing Cracow, the last of the Confederate strongholds, and thenceforward Turkey had to face the Russians unaided. The war was one-sided. By the end of 1769 the Russians were in control of Moldavia, Wallachia and the Crimea. And a large fleet, manned and guided by English sailors and officers, though nominally under the command of Gregory Orloff, entered the Aegean, destroyed the Turkish fleet at Tchesmé and incited an insurrection in Greece.

The rapid success of the Russians along the Danube roused the court of Austria and even caused Russia's ally, Frederick, to grow anxious at the extension of Muscovite power. Joseph II. and Frederick met in conference at Neustadt in Moravia in 1770, and Kaunitz pressed the King of Prussia to join Austria in opposing Russian ambition by force of arms if necessary. Frederick had long been meditating the annexation of Polish Prussia, which divided his dominions, but he knew that he could not accomplish it without the concurrence of Austria and Russia. The jealousies of the European states during the eighteenth century, and especially those of Austria, Russia and Prussia, forbade that any of them should expand unless the others should be indemnified, lest the balance of power might be destroyed. As they could not expand separately, they must expand together; and this situation explains the various treaties of alliance and partition of that century. It was at the Neustadt meeting [1] that Frederick suggested to Kaunitz the dismemberment of Poland and the plan of compelling Russia to seek indemnity in Poland instead of retaining Moldavia and Wallachia. While the conference was in session messengers arrived from Constantinople begging the two monarchs to mediate between Russia and Turkey, and the conference broke up with the understanding that Frederick was to use his good offices with Catherine.

[1] Coxe, *History of the House of Austria*, chap. cxix.

Austria never had a more able or more devoted servant than Count, afterwards Prince Kaunitz, and he was not likely to leave anything undone that would redound to the glory of the House of Hapsburg. When therefore the Turks proposed to Austria in 1771 an alliance against Russia, and offered most advantageous terms, Kaunitz accepted the overture in spite of his conversations with Frederick of the previous summer; and on July 6, 1771, a defensive and offensive alliance was made [1] whereby, in return for the restoration to the Porte of all the territory that had been conquered by Russia, Turkey was to cede Little Wallachia to Austria, to free Austrian commerce from all taxes and to pay Austria an annual subsidy of ten thousand florins in four installments, the first of which was actually paid. Murray, the English ambassador at Constantinople, obtained a copy of the treaty, and communicated it to Berlin and St. Petersburg. By this time Frederick had matured his plan for Polish dismemberment, and he sent his brother, Prince Henry, to St. Petersburg to persuade Catharine to relinquish her designs on Turkey and seek compensation in Poland. Frederick enlarged upon the dangers to Russia of the alliance of the Porte with Austria, and assured Catharine that France would certainly aid the latter country. He pointed out that the indemnification which Catherine could justly claim for the expenses of the existing war might readily be obtained in Poland, but that in order to maintain the balance of power in eastern Europe it would be necessary for both Austria and Prussia to enlarge their boundaries. The plan was not at all relished by Count Panin and the Russian court, for the simple reason that knowing their influence was supreme in Poland, they were averse to sharing with others what they desired to obtain for themselves alone. But Catherine was frightened at the Austro-Turkish alliance and proposed to Frederick a counter-alliance, by which they

---

[1] According to Martens, *Recueil des Principaux Traités*, vol. vi, p. 134, the treaty was not ratified.

should reciprocally guarantee their possessions and pledge themselves to assist each other against Austria in case of war. Frederick agreed to this proposal on the promise of Russia that she would relinquish Moldavia and Wallachia, and thus avoid giving to Austria a cause for quarrel.[1] At the same time Catherine entered into an armistice with Turkey, and the most of 1772 was spent in negotiations at Fokschani and Bucharest.

Having succeeded at St. Petersburg, Frederick again turned to Vienna, where he encountered much difficulty. Kaunitz set great store by the Turkish alliance, provided Prussia would remain neutral; and Maria Theresa, of whom Frederick said that she was always weeping and always grabbing, had scruples about the Polish spoliation. Frederick, who was anxious to settle the matter, refused to promise neutrality; on the contrary, he began to mobilize his troops. This alarmed Kaunitz, who soon convinced Maria Theresa that there would be less effusion of blood in accepting territory in Poland than in fighting for it along the Danube.[2] The three courts, therefore, came to an agreement as to their shares of the spoil by the first Treaty of Partition, July 25, 1772,[3] and Turkey, who had refused to come to terms, was once more left to her fate. Early in 1773 the Russian ultimatum was delivered at the conference of Bucharest. It required that the Crimea should be an independent Tartar state under the protection of Russia, and that the two principal fortresses of Kertsh and Yenikalie should remain in Russian hands; that Russian ships, naval as well as merchant, should enjoy the free navigation of the Black Sea and the Archipelago; that Russia should have a permanent resident at Constantinople, and that the sovereign of Russia should receive the title of

[1] Schöll, *Histoire des Traités de Paix*, vol. xiv, p. 36.

[2] For a history of the Polish dismemberment see *Von Hammer*, vol. viii, books 61 and 62 *passim*.

[3] Martens, *Recueil des Traités*, vol. ii, p. 89.

Padishah; and that Russia should have the right to protect
the Christian inhabitants of the Ottoman Empire who professed the Greek religion.   Severe as these demands were, the
Sultan, his councillors and his generals, advised their acceptance, so weakened had Turkey become.   France also advised
the Turks to end the war, it being evident that she could not
help them without incurring the hostility of most of Europe.
But the Ulema and Softas [1] were obdurate, and the Sultan felt
that to act contrary to their wishes would produce an insurrection and probably lead to his own deposition.   Negotiations
consequently were broken off and hostilities were resumed
early in 1773.

Though at first successful, the Turks soon met with repeated
defeats, and again became anxious for peace.   Nor were the
Russians less anxious.   Their losses during the war had been
tremendous; it was evident that the Poles intended to rise
against the Partition Treaty; but above all, in 1773, the im-
postor Pugatcheff, who impersonated the murdered Peter III.,
raised a formidable insurrection which spread desolation
through southern and eastern Russia.   When, therefore, Suwarrow surrounded the Turks at Shumla, the Russians, although they denied a request for an armistice, urged the grand
vizier to send plenipotentiaries to treat for peace.   The conference took place at Kutchonc-Kainardji, in the tent of the Russian General, July 17, 1774, and resulted in the famous compact known as the Treaty of Kainardji.   The text of the
treaty [2] is in Italian.[3]   The negotiations were conducted with
military celerity.   The basis of the peace was the Russian
ultimatum presented at Bucharest in 1772, and an agreement

---

[1] The Softas are the theological students.   With the Ulema they form a bulwark
against all reforms or innovations.

[2] Martens, *Recueil des Traités*, vol. ii, p. 286.

[3] Negotiations with the Ottoman Porte were frequently in Italian.   As late as
1761 the treaty of commerce with Prussia was in that language.   In the Egyptian mixed judicial tribunals of to-day Italian is one of the official languages.

was reached in seven hours; but the Russians, with a view to
vaunt their triumph, delayed the signature four days till July
21st, the anniversary of the peace of the Pruth.   The advantages which Russia gained by the treaty were far-reaching.
" The two empires have agreed to annihilate and leave in an
eternal oblivion all the treaties and conventions heretofore
made between the two states . . . and never to put forward
any claim grounded upon the said conventions." [1]   The Ottoman Porte agreed that the Tartars of the Crimea, Kuban and
adjacent regions, between the rivers Berda and Dneiper, and
also the inhabitants of territories lying between the Bug and
Dniester, as far as the frontier of Poland, should form an independent state, and that "Neither the court of Russia nor the
Ottoman shall interfere under any pretext whatever with the
election of the said Khan, or in the domestic, political, civil
and internal affairs of the said state."   But within the boundaries of this newly organized Tartar state, Russia retained for
herself the fortresses of Kertsch and Yenikalie in the Crimea,
the city of Azof and its district, and the castle of Kilburn at
the mouth of the Dneiper, with a district along the left bank
of the Dneiper.[2]   Moldavia, Wallachia and Bessarabia were
given back to the Ottoman Porte on condition of " a grant of
an amnesty for all offenses during the war; free exercise of
the Christian religion and permission from the Porte that according as the circumstances of those two principalities may
require, the ministers of the imperial court of Russia resident
at Constantinople may remonstrate in their favor." [3]   A very
important clause of the treaty (article 7) respecting the Christian subjects of the Sultan declared: " The sublime Porte

---

[1] It is for this reason that the Turkish question of the nineteenth century dates
from the Treaty of Kainardji, all the Russian claims being founded upon it and
almost every treaty thereafter confirming it.

[2] All this was merely a step in the direction of incorporation into Russia.

[3] All of which would tend to cause the Christian population of these territories
to look to Russia in the future as their sovereign, instead of Turkey.

promises to protect constantly the Christian religion and its churches, and it also allows the imperial court of Russia to make upon all occasions representations as well in favor of the new church at Constantinople, of which mention will be made in article 14, as on behalf of its officiating ministers." [1] The words referred to in the fourteenth article were: " After the manner of the other powers permission is given to the high court of Russia in addition to the chapel built in the minister's residence, to erect in one of the quarters of Galata, in the street called Bey Oglu, a public church in which the Christians may worship according to the Greek ritual, which shall always be under the protection of the ministers of that empire and secure from coercion and outrage." The straits were to be opened to the merchant ships of both parties, and Russian merchant-men were to be treated in the same way as the French, who were then the most favored nation. Russia also obtained the right to have resident consuls in all parts of the Turkish Empire. Turkey agreed to permit the residence of a Russian minister at Constantinople, and to give the Russian sovereign the title of Padishah, " which had hitherto been refused." Not a word was said about Poland, although the Russian treatment of Poland had been one of the causes of the war. The general opinion in the European chancelleries, as well as among the learned of Europe, was that the Ottoman Empire had received a blow from which it would never be able to recover. Even many French statesmen believed that it would be impossible for France to support the Ottoman Empire any longer, and that it behooved France to consider its early demise, and prepare to share in its effects. The treaty gave a great blow to French prestige in the East. Russia had the advantage of position, race and religion, and gradually supplanted France in the exercise of special privileges of protec-

---

[1] It is upon this clause that Russia, in 1853, founded their claim to the general protection of all the inhabitants of the Ottoman Empire who were members of the Orthodox Church.

tion.   The treaty was acclaimed by the Voltaireans and En-
cyclopedists, who were addicted to magnifying the word and
worth of Catherine II., and who dreamed of the re-establishment of the Greek Empire.   Immediately after the signing of
the treaty, Austria occupied the Bukovina, which Turkey was
compelled to cede to her by the Treaty of Constantinople of
May 7, 1775.[1]

[1] Neumann, *Recueil des Traités conclus par l'Autriche*, vol. i, p. 173.   This
causes the friction between Austro-Hungary and Roumania to-day.   The Bukovina is inhabited almost entirely by a Roumanian people, who are anxious to unite
with Roumania.

CHAPTER III

RUSSIAN AGGRESSION

DURING the second part of her reign Catharine II. abandoned the System of the North, *i. e.*, the alliance with Prussia
and England against France and Austria, and became recon-
ciled with the two latter countries, and especially with Austria.
Catherine and her counsellors had decided on their plan for
Ottoman dismemberment, but needed an ally in central
Europe for its fulfillment; and the character of Joseph II. in-
dicated him as the proper one. Panin was gradually supplanted in power by Potemkin, and in the latter the Ottoman
Empire found an implacable enemy. He had never intended
that the provisions of the Treaty of Kainardji relating to the
new Tartar State should be carried into effect, and as soon as
the Pugatcheff rebellion was suppressed, he inaugurated in the
Crimea the policy which had proved to be so successful in
Poland. Russian intrigues secured the election of Sahim
Gherai as the new Khan, and at the same time instigated his
subjects to revolt against him beeause of his partiality to
Russian customs.[1] In 1777 he found it necessary to call in
the aid of his creator, and the Russian army penetrated into
the Crimea and suppressed the rebellion. The Ottoman Porte
was indignant at this violation of the Treaty of Kainardji, but
Potemkin had selected a most opportune moment. War was
about to break out between France and England over the
American question. Joseph II. had been completely won
over to Catherine's views with regard to the Ottoman Empire,
and Frederick the Great did not dare oppose Russia unsup-

[1] *Annual Register for 1778.*

ported. Upon the advice of France, therefore, the Ottoman Porte remained passive, and in 1779 a convention was signed between Russia and Turkey by which not only the provisions of the Treaty of Kainardji were confirmed, but by which Russia obtained substantial privileges in the navigation of the Black Sea, while the authority of the Ottoman Porte in the principalities was much diminished and Potemkin's tool, Sahim Gherai, was recognized as Khan of the Crimea.[1]

In 1782 the rebellion instigated by Potemkin's agents broke out again; and Catherine and Potemkin determined to take advantage of the opportunity to carry out their long cherished scheme. The Crimea was again invaded, the Khan deposed and the world notified that the independent Tartar State had been annexed to Russia. A manifesto[2] was published April 3, 1783, professing the same ground of intervention as in the case of Poland, viz., the benefits to be conferred on the Tartar people by the suppression of civil war and anarchy. The Turks were indignant and threatened war, but Vergennes, who was then Louis XVI's chief minister, restrained them. He could obtain support against Russia nowhere.[3] Joseph II. was altogether committed to the Russian programme by the Treaty of 1781.[4] Frederick was hoping to get the Polish cities of Thorn and Dantzig, and therefore could not afford to alienate Russia; besides, he objected to the treaty of alliance between France and Austria of 1756. Even before the definitive Treaty of Paris of 1783 was signed, Vergennes turned to England, but Fox, who was then secretary of state for foreign affairs, distinctly avowed his preference for Russia,[5]

---

[1] Martens, *Recueil des Principaux Traités*, vol iii, p. 349.

[2] *Ibid.*, vol. iv, p. 444.

[3] Flassan, *Diplomatie Française*, vol. vii, book 8, containing the memoire of Vergennes to Louis XVI. suggesting measures to be taken in agreement with other courts to prevent the Russian aggression.

[4] Martens, *Recueil des Traités conclus par la Russie*, vol. ii, p. 96.

[5] See Fox's admission in Hansard's *Parliamentary Debates*, vol. xxix, p. 63.

and England could hardly be expected to support France in anything after the latter's assistance to her revolted colonies. The only sovereign apparently in a position to help Turkey was Gustavus III. of Sweden, but in the very year 1783 he was obliged to come to terms with Catherine. The Turks could do nothing but follow the advice of France and submit to the humiliation. On January 8, 1784, through the mediation of M. St. Priest, the French ambassador, there was signed the Treaty of Constantinople,[1] by which the Ottoman Porte, although confirmed in the possession of Oczakof and its territory, acknowledged the annexation both of the Crimea and Kuban to Russia.

After the annexation of the Crimea, Catherine made little secret of her intentions with reference to the Ottoman Empire, and she subordinated everything else to her policy in regard to that state. In her triumphal progress to her new territories, in 1787, she was met at Cherson by Joseph II., and conferences took place as to the fate of the Turk. Catherine II.'s grandson, who had just been born, was named Constantine; a triumphal arch was erected at Cherson, with the inscription, " This is the way to Byzantium;" and there was open talk of the re-establishment of the Greek Empire under a Russian Prince, with compensation to Austria in Servia and Dalmatia.[2] All this was sufficiently irritating to the Turk, but evidence soon accumulated that the Russian consuls at Jassy, Bucharest, Smyrna, Alexandria and elsewhere, who had been forced upon the Ottoman Porte by the Treaty of Kainardji, were inciting rebellion. In the face of all these provocations, the Porte, unable to withstand the indignation of the populace of Constantinople, declared war against Russia, August 15, 1787.

[1] Martens, *Recueil des Principaux Traités*, vol. ii, p. 505.

[2] Arneth's *Joseph II. und Katharina von Russland*, containing the letter of Catherine to Joseph of September 10, 1782, and the answer of Joseph of November 13, in which the views of the two monarchs as to the partition of the Ottoman Empire are set forth in full.

This was what Catherine desired, for by the Treaty of 1781, Russia and Austria were bound to aid each other only in case they were attacked, and Catherine hoped, by making the Porte appear to be the aggressor, to induce Joseph II. to form an offensive as well as defensive alliance. The Turks made a dignified appeal to Joseph, reminding him that when they had been invited to participate in the dismemberment of the Austrian possessions, at the accession of Maria Theresa, they had refused.[1] But Joseph was anxious to share in the conquest, and war was declared by Austria and Russia against Turkey, in February, 1788.

Although Frederick the Great was dead, his anti-Austrian policy was continued by his old minister, Count Herzberg, who was retained by Frederick William II. in the early days of his reign; and in 1788[2] an alliance was formed between Prussia and England,[3] which, although immediately directed against French intervention in the Netherlands, was also designed to thwart the schemes of Austria and Russia with reference to the Ottoman Empire.[4] The allies roused the enemies of Russia and Austria to activity. They supported the Belgian revolt against Joseph in the Netherlands; they assisted Sweden in the war which she began against Russia, and compelled Denmark to withhold from the latter the aid which she intended to give; they encouraged Poland in reforms antagonistic to Russia. Nevertheless, although at first unsuccessful, the Austrians penetrated into Servia and the Russians into the principalities, so that it looked once more as if the Ottoman Empire were doomed. Prussia then concluded, January 31, 1790, a treaty[5]

---

[1] Coxe, *History of the House of Austria*, vol. iii, p. 516.

[2] For evidence of the intense hatred which existed between the courts of Vienna and Berlin, *Malmesbury's Diaries*, vol. iii, p. 34. Though this refers to 1793, the feeling was a survival of that engendered by Frederick the Great.

[3] Martens, *Recueil des Principaux Traités*, vol. iii, p. 146.

[4] Hansard's *Parliamentary Debates*, vol. xxix, p. 79.

[5] Martens, *Recueil des Principaux Traités*, vol. iv, p. 560.

with the Porte, by which she agreed to guarantee to the Sultan the full and unimpaired possession of his dominions as against Austria. This treaty, however, was not destined to be executed, for on February 20, 1790, Joseph II. died. The radical reforms which he had instituted in his dominions had produced wide-spread revolt, especially among those whom they were intended to benefit, and he was compelled to call many of his best troops from the front. At the time of his decease, Prussia was seeking to obtain the Polish seaports of Thorn and Dantzig, in return for which she offered to recover Galicia from Austria and restore it to Poland; and with this in view, she stationed troops along the frontiers of Siberia and Galicia. Under these circumstances, the new Emperor, Leopold II., decided to come to terms with the Turks. It was his policy to placate England, and to prepare to fight Prussia if necessary. He also alarmed England by threatening to cede the Austrian Netherlands to France. England, therefore, agreed to the Congress of Reichenbach. Leopold understood better than Joseph had done the danger of having a Russian at Constantinople; and at the Congress [1] he agreed to lend no further aid to Russia against the Turks and to restore to the Belgians their hereditary rights and privileges. England was thereby satisfied, while Herzberg was thwarted. In consequence of this arrangement, an armistice was declared between Austria and Turkey, and after long discussion, the Treaty of Sistova [2] was signed between the two countries, August 4, 1791. By it Turkey lost only the town of Old Orsova and the territory of the Unna.

Russia, who had then concluded peace with Sweden, remained unmoved by the threats made at Reichenbach, and continued at war with the Turks, repeatedly defeating them in battle. A Russian fleet was also got ready in the Baltic to

---

[1] Martens, *Recueil des Principaux Traités*, vol. iii, p. 170.

[2] Neumann, *Recueil des Traités conclus par l'Autriche*, vol. i, p. 454.

renew the enterprise of Gregory Orloff, namely, to sail to
Greece and rouse the inhabitants. But the younger Pitt was
now prime minister of England, and he inaugurated the policy
which afterwards became traditional in English diplomacy, of
maintaining the integrity of the Ottoman Empire as a necessary condition of the preservation of the balance of power.
An English fleet was prepared for service in the Baltic, though
the idea of a war with Russia at that time was rendered unpopular by the exertions of Fox and Burke and the opposition
of the mercantile class who feared the loss of the Baltic trade.[1]
Prussia placed a large army on foot and also offered mediation, but Catherine was incensed and declined it. It was the
changed condition of Poland that impelled Catherine to agree
to a peace, the conclusion of which was facilitated by the death
of Potemkin, who had opposed it. Kosciusko and his com-
patriots had made excellent reforms, both political and military, and it was evident to Catherine that she would need
Suwarrow and his veterans in Poland, if she was to carry out
her schemes of further Polish dismemberment. Once more
Poland was to be the ransom of Turkey. Catherine accepted
the mediation of Denmark, who was friendly to Russia, and on
January 9, 1792, the Treaty of Jassy[2] was signed. By it the
western boundary of Russia was extended to the Dniester;
and all the coast of the Black Sea between the Bug and the
Dniester, with the fortress of Oczakof, became Russian. Stipulations in favor of the Danubian principalities were also made,
requiring the Ottoman Porte to lighten the burdens of their
inhabitants in various ways.

The condition of the Ottoman Empire in the years succeed-
ing the Peace of Jassy was truly deplorable. Anarchy reigned
everywhere, and the pashas made themselves practically inde-

---

[1] The attitude of the various English statesmen on the Eastern question at this
time is fully shown in Hansard's *Parliamentary Debates*, vol. xxix *passim*.

[2] Martens, *Recueil des Principaux Traités*, vol. v, p. 67.

pendent.[1] Even before the Revolution a party in France had
maintained that French interests would be better served in
agreeing to the dismemberment of the Ottoman Empire than
in maintaining its integrity.[2] The series of unsuccessful wars
fought by Turkey and the resulting confusion in internal administration led many French statesmen to believe that dissolution was inevitable, and that France should look to receiving her share. It was a cherished tradition of the French
foreign office that if the Ottoman Empire should ever be dismembered Egypt should fall to the lot of France.[3] This view
was retained by the French Directory, which besides was
anxious to get rid of a too successful general; and it was also
shared by that general himself, who believed that one of the
surest ways of striking at England was by way of India.
Negotiations were therefore opened with Tippoo Tib and the
other Indian princes opposed to England, and great preparations were made for a naval expedition, the destination of
which was kept secret. The French set sail from Toulon
May 19, 1798, took Malta on the way from the Knights of St.
John, landed in Egypt and defeated the Mamelukes in the
Battle of the Pyramids. The news of the expedition was received in Constantinople with stupefaction. The ally, whom
the Ottoman Porte had been accustomed to consult for more
than two hundred years, had betrayed it. The astonishment,
however, was equalled by the indignation. Nor could the
French explanation that they were making war only upon the
rebellious Mamelukes, who had interfered with French com-

---

[1] The opportunity for ending the contest with the Ottoman Empire was not open
to either Austria or Russia. The former was engaged with Bonaparte in Italy;
the latter was trying to pacify and assimilate Poland. Catherine was, however,
on the eve of beginning hostilities in 1796 when she died. Eton, *Survey of the
Turkish Empire*, p. 451 *et seq.*

[2] *Annual Register for 1798*, p. 135.

[3] Memoire addressed by Leibnitz to Louis XIV, January, 1672, in De Testa,
Recueil des Traités de la Porte Ottomane, vol. i, p. 525.

merce, and that they were fighting *for* the Sultan and *not* against him, blind the Turks to the true significance of the invasion. The Russian and English ambassadors were there to enlighten them. A Djihad, or Holy War, was proclaimed against the French. Ruffin, the French chargé d'affaires, was thrown into the Seven Towers, the French mercantile establishments were destroyed and the religious orders dispersed. War was declared September 12, 1798, and an alliance was concluded with Russia December 23,[1] to which England acceded January 5, 1799. The French, though at first successful in Egypt, were eventually compelled to surrender to the English, and a combined Russian and Turkish fleet took from them the Ionian Islands, which had been given to them under the Treaty of Campo Formio.[2]

On the conclusion of the Peace of Amiens between France and England, a treaty of peace was also signed between France and Turkey, January 25, 1802.[3] By this treaty the Ottoman Porte was confirmed in its possession of Egypt and all its territories. In return the property confiscated by the Porte from the French mercantile and religious establishments was restored, and the capitulations of 1740 were renewed with new stipulations, giving French ships the right to enter the Black Sea and navigate there without restriction. The Ionian Islands were erected into an independent republic, and the Greek inhabitants were permitted to choose their own protector. They naturally chose the Emperor of Russia. Immediately after the conclusion of peace Napoleon resumed the old policy of courting the friendship of the Porte, and so skillful were the French ambassadors, especially General Sebastiani, that in a few years France had regained all her old influence over the Divan.

[1] Martens, *Recueil des Principaux Traités*, vol. vii, p. 256.

[2] De Clerq, *Recueil des Traités de la France*, vol. i, p. 335, art. 5.

[3] For documents relating to the French expedition to Egypt, *Correspondence de Napoléon I*, nos. 2500–4400. Also De Testa, *Recueil des Traités de la Porte Ottomane*, vol. i, pp. 495 *et seq.*

For some time, however, the Porte continued to lean on its
allies of the late war, England and Russia. By a convention
concluded with Russia, September 24, 1802, the Sultan agreed
not to remove the hospodars of Moldavia and Wallachia
without the consent of Russia, nor to allow any Turks, except
merchants, to enter either principality. A naval station was
also conceded to Russia on the southern shore of the Black
Sea, and the Russian fleets were allowed to pass and repass
the Dardanelles. In 1803 the Servians rose under Kara
George, and massacred the Janissaries, who had nowhere been
so tyrannical as in Servia, where they plundered and murdered
the rayahs without restraint. The rising took place with the
permission, and even at the instigation, of the Sultan; but
later, when he ordered the Servians to return to their homes,
they refused to do so until reforms had been granted.[1] Following the example of the Roumanians they sent a deputation
in August, 1804, to St. Petersburg. The deputation was well
received. The Russian emperor advised the Servians to present their request to the Porte, and promised to support it.
In the summer of 1805, therefore, a Servian deputation went
to Constantinople and demanded that in future all Servian
fortresses should be garrisoned by Servian troops, and that in
consideration of the unsettled condition of the country, the
arrears of taxes and tribute should not be exacted. This
demand was made at a crisis in the history of Turkey.[2]
Sultan Selim was making every effort to reorganize his empire
and introduce reforms, but the Janissaries were in a dangerous
mood because of the treatment of their brethren in Servia; nor
could he rely upon the aid of the Divan, whose members were
little more than pensioners either of France or of Russia.
The French ambassador, Marshal Brune, demanded that the
Sultan recognize the new French Empire, and give Napoleon
the title of Padishah; the British and Russian ambassadors

[1] Ranke, *History of Servia*, chaps. vi–xviii.

[2] *Annual Register for 1806*, pp. 21 *et seq.*

threatened to leave Constantinople if he did. Finally, when the coalition of 1805 was about to attack Napoleon, the Russian ambassador, Italinzki, demanded that the Porte form an offensive and defensive alliance with Russia against France· This demand was made at the same time that the Servian delegation presented its petition at Constantinople. The Sultan deemed it necessary to temporize with Russia, who had one army along the Danube, another in the Ionian Islands, and a third in the Crimea; and he entered into negotiations with Italinzki; but he determined to act promptly against the Servians. Their demands were rejected and their deputation thrown into the Seven Towers, while two Ottoman armies were sent against Kara George. But the Servians had learned to fight in the armies of Joseph II., and a national spirit had been developed in their struggles with the Janissaries. The Ottoman forces were defeated, the Turkish fortresses in Servia were captured, and the Servians by their own efforts and without foreign assistance won their independence in 1806. In the mean time Napoleon had captured the Austrian army at Ulm and had defeated the combined Austrians and Russians at Austerlitz. This necessitated the withdrawal of the Russian forces along the Danube and in the Crimea, and relieved Turkey from pressure in that quarter. The French ambassador placed the Treaty of Pressbourg, which Napoleon had concluded with Austria, before the Divan. By this treaty France obtained Dalmatia and Illyria, and thus became a neighbor of Turkey. This circumstance was by no means pleasing to the Porte, but the Sultan, desirous of retaining the friendship of France, bestowed upon Napoleon by a Hatti-sheriff the title of Padishah, and sent an extraordinary embassy to Paris. Sebastiani was sent to Constantinople in return, to reorganize the Turkish army.

Sebastiani soon acquired great influence with the Divan, and he used it to excellent purpose for his master. Russia and Prussia had declared war against Napoleon in September,

1806, and it was important that a diversion should be made
along the Danube in order to prevent the entire Russian
strength from being concentrated in Poland.   Sebastiani
journeyed through the principalities, and on his return convinced the Sultan that Ypsilanti and Morouzi, the hospodars
of Wallachia and Moldavia, were really agents of Russia and
traitors to Turkey.   The Sultan dismissed them both, in defiance of the convention of 1802 ; but upon the demand of the
British and Russian ambassadors, backed by a threat of force,
reinstated them.   The Russians nevertheless crossed the Pruth
and occupied the principalities.   This act excited the jealousy
of Austria, and was one of the principal reasons why Austria
did not join the coalition of 1806 against Napoleon, who on
more than one occasion employed the differences among the
various European powers as to the partition of the Ottoman
Empire for the purpose of dividing his enemies.[1]   The Ottoman Porte declared war against Russia December 30, 1806,
notwithstanding the menaces of Arbuthnot, the British minister.   The British fleet was ordered to sail against Constantinople, and on February 19, 1807, favored by a strong wind,
it passed through the Dardanelles and the Sea of Marmora
and anchored off Princess' Island near Constantinople.   The
Divan was terrified, and was disposed to yield to Arbuthnot's
ultimatum that Sebastiani be immediately sent away from
Constantinople, that the alliance with Russia and England be
renewed, and that the Straits be opened to the Russian fleets.
But Sebastiani animated the Turks with his own courage, and
while the Divan trifled with Arbuthnot through notes dictated
by the French ambassador, the latter displayed the greatest
activity in repairing the fortifications of the city, so that when
the Divan gave its refusal to the ultimatum, Admiral Duck-
worth found the defenses too strong to be taken and sailed
back through the Dardanelles with considerable loss.   He
afterwards landed an expedition in Egypt, which was unsuc-

[1] Vandal, *Napoléon et Alexandre I*, vol. i, chap. preliminaire.

cessful, so that in the South during 1807 the Turks did not
fare so badly. In the North very little was done by either
side. The Russians were obliged to give their attention to
their more formidable enemy, Napoleon, and could oppose to
the Turks only such troops as they could spare. The Turks
on the other hand were distracted by revolts in the army and
by uprisings among the people. Early in May, 1807, Sultan
Selim was deposed by the Janissaries, and Mustapha IV was
placed upon the throne. Napoleon used this as a pretext for
abandoning Turkey to Russia in the Treaty of Tilsit, July 7,
1807.[1] The public articles referring to Turkey provided that
the Russians should evacuate Moldavia and Wallachia, but
that the Turks should not enter the principalities until a treaty
of peace should be made between the two countries.[2] General
Guillemont, the French agent, negotiated a cessation of hostilities between Russia and Turkey at Slobosia in August,
1807. It was agreed between Alexander and Napoleon, however, that the stipulations of Tilsit with reference to the evacuation of the principalities, should be practically disregarded,
and article 8 of the secret alliance provided that if the Porte
should not comply with the recommendations of France and
Russia, her European possessions, except Constantinople and
Roumelia, " should be withdrawn from the vexation of the
Turkish government." The Turks knew nothing of the secret
articles, but they were sufficiently astonished by the public
articles. They had been led to expect the recovery of the
Crimea; instead they saw the principalities remain in the
hands of the enemy. General Sebastiani's position became so
embarrassing in Constantinople after the signature of the
treaty that he obtained his recall.

The retention of the principalities by Russia caused the
greatest uneasiness at Vienna, and the Austrian government
used its best efforts to bring about a reconciliation between

[1] Vandal, *Napoléon et Alexandre I*, vol. i, chap. 1.

[2] De Clercq, *Recueil des Traités de la France*, vol. ii, p. 207, arts. 22 and 23.

Turkey and England, so that the latter might act as a protectress of Turkey against the designs which were believed to have been formed at Tilsit and Erfurt. At the conference of Erfurt, Napoleon, who foresaw trouble with Austria and was thus doubly anxious to retain the alliance with Russia, made greater concessions to Alexander than at Tilsit.[1] By a treaty which was to remain a "plus profond secret," October 12, 1808, he recognized the Czar's possession of Moldavia and Wallachia, and also of Finland, which the Russians had just torn from Sweden; and the two monarchs agreed not to treat with England unless " she should agree to recognize Moldavia, Wallachia and Finland as part of the Russian Empire." The English ministry obtained knowledge of the treaty and accepted the good offices of Austria in bringing about a reconciliation with Turkey. January 15, 1809, Sir Robt. Adair concluded the Peace of the Dardanelles.[2] This was highly displeasing both to France and to Russia. Napoleon was especially incensed at Austria. He ascribed the treaty to Austrian intrigues, and it was one of the causes of the war between France and Austria a few months later.[3] The menaces of France and Russia and the continued occupation of the principalities by the Russians brought about in March, 1809, the renewal of the hostilities, which had been suspended since the armistice of Slobosia. During 1809 and 1810 the Russians were almost completely successful; but in the mean time Napoleon and Alexander had become estranged and were preparing for the conflict which seemed inevitable. The Russians, therefore, in 1811, withdrew a large part of their forces from the Danube to strengthen the army which was to operate against Napoleon, and in the war with Turkey acted entirely on the defensive. The English minister zealously encouraged

[1] De Clercq, *Recueil des Traités de la France*, vol. ii, p. 284, arts. 8 and 9.

[2] Martens, *Nouveau Recueil des Principaux Traités*, vol. i, p. 160.

[3] As to difficulties attending the conclusion of the Peace of the Dardanelles, see Adair, *Mission to Constantinople*.

the reconciliation of Russia and Turkey in order to give a free hand to Alexander against Napoleon, and persuaded the former to abate his demands. Napoleon, on the other hand, made desperate efforts to regain the confidence of the Turks, and urged them to commence active operations along the Danube, promising them that he would make no treaty with Russia which did not provide for the restoration of Moldavia, Wallachia and the Crimea. But his secret agreement at Tilsit for the dismemberment of Turkey was laid before the Divan; and the resentment and distrust thus aroused, together with the liberal use of money, induced the Ottoman Porte to agree, May 28, 1812, to the Treaty of Bucharest.[1] The Russian army, which was thereby released, hurried towards Moscow and materially assisted in the destruction of the French. By the treaty of Bucharest, Moldavia and Wallachia were restored to the Porte, but Bessarabia was given to Russia. The Russian boundary was thus moved westward to the Pruth, and the Sulina mouth of the Danube became Russian. The Porte moreover bound itself to maintain and respect forever certain stipulations in favor of the inhabitants of the princi-palities; to demand no taxes for the period of the war and for two years afterwards; and to allow four months for any of the inhabitants to emigrate. Article 8 returned Servia to the Porte, with the reservation that there was to be a general amnesty. The administration of their internal affairs was to be left to the Servians, but the fortresses were to be occupied by Turkish garrisons. It is significant that this treaty was concluded through the instrumentality of Stratford Canning, who was afterward to occupy so large a place in Ottoman history.[2]

[1] Martens, *Nouveau Recueil des Traités*, vol. iii, p. 397.

[2] Lane Poole, *Life of Stratford Canning*, chap. iv.

CHAPTER IV

THE GREEK REVOLUTION

No representative of the Ottoman Porte was admitted to the Congress of Vienna, and in the proceedings of the Congress the Sultan found grave cause for apprehension. The engagements of the allies extended to practically all Europe except the Ottoman Empire; and when the question of its territorial integrity was brought up for discussion, the Emperor Alexander refused to allow it to be considered.[1] The Porte also looked with much suspicion upon the Holy Alliance. This alliance, which was formed at the instance of Alexander, purported to regard the various states of Europe as members of one "*Christian nation*, to be governed according to the teachings of Christ;" and the Sultan was not invited to adhere, as were all other European monarchs. Moreover, Alexander surrounded himself with avowed enemies of Turkey. One of his ministers of foreign affairs was the Greek Capodistrias; the Ypsilanti brothers, sons of the former hospodar of Moldavia were officers in the Russian army and friends of the Czar. The Hetairia, the Greek revolutionary society, was founded in Russia, whence it was permitted to carry on its propagandism. Nor were these the only ways in which Alexander exhibited his enmity to Turkey. In 1816, he proposed to the powers that if the Ottoman Porte could not suppress the Barbary pirates, all Europe should make a crusade against them. By the advice of England and Austria, who were determined to uphold the integrity of the Ottoman Empire, the Porte endeavored in every way to avoid giving offense. This circum-

[1] Seignobos, *Political History of Europe since 1814*, chap. xxv.

stance chiefly explains the favorable terms granted to the Servians, who again revolted under Miloch Obrenovitch, in 1815.
By the compact of 1817, Miloch was recognized as knès or
prince superior of Servia; and although Turkish garrisons
were retained in the fortresses, a large measure of local autonomy was granted to the Servians.

Indeed, the avoidance of trouble with foreign powers was
then essential to the safety of Turkey. Never was the country
in a worse state of anarchy. Mehemet Ali had made himself
practically independent in Egypt; the fanatic Wahabites were
in possession of the Holy Places in Arabia; Ali Pasha of
Janina ruled as a sovereign prince in Epirus and defiantly
contemned the commands of the Sultan, while his example
was, to some extent, imitated by the provincial pashas; the
rayahs were in revolt in several provinces, and the Janissaries
were rebellious. Few monarchs faced, in the decade succeed-
ing the Congress of Vienna, conditions more untoward than
those that surrounded Mahmoud II; but he was a man of
resolute energy, and set about systematically to recover his
lost authority throughout the empire. The most serious ob-
stacle to this was Ali Pasha of Janina, and his destruction was
determined upon. For some years Ali treated lightly the
attacks made upon him, but when, in 1820, Mahmoud made
immense preparations for his destruction, he sought to obtain
the support of the Christian rayahs of Greece, and incited
them to revolt.[1]

The Greeks had made remarkable progress in wealth, in-
telligence and national spirit since the Peace of Kainardji.
That peace had compelled the Ottoman Porte to receive
Russian consuls in the various cities and ports, and these were
nearly all Greeks. During the French Revolution and
Napoleonic struggles almost the entire trade of the Levant

---

[1] For the condition of the Ottoman Empire previous to the Greek Revolution
consult the *Annuaire Lesur* for 1818, chap. iv; 1819, chap. vi; 1820, chap. xi,
and 1821, chaps. vi–viii.

and a large part of the trade of the Mediterranean fell into the hands of the Greeks, sailing as they did under the neutral flag of Turkey. Few Turks engaged in commerce. It is estimated that the maritime population of Greece in 1815 numbered twenty-five thousand men, and that more than five hundred ships were owned by Greeks. The new class of merchants and traders sent their sons to be educated in France, England and Germany, and these young men, when they returned to their homes, were not only unwilling to exhibit in their attitude toward the Ottoman Porte the servility displayed by the Greek clergy, but they began to dispute with the latter for supremacy in the nation. It was principally from their ranks that the Hetairia was recruited, an association which developed from a literary into a political society, whose object was the emancipation of Hellas. Uprisings took place simultaneously in the Morea, in the archipelago and in the Danubian principalities. The revolt in the principalities was a failure. The Roumanians in reality felt little interest in the fate of Greece. Ypsilanti was driven by the Turkish troops into Austria, where he was interned by Metternich as a revolutionist. But the insurrection in Greece was everywhere successful, and the massacres of Christians which took place all over Turkey, beginning with the hanging of the patriarch in his robes from the gate of his own church at Constantinople, aroused the indignation of Europe and created an intense sympathy with the Greek cause.[1]

The Greeks naturally looked to Alexander for encouragement and support, but Alexander had gone through a peculiar evolution since 1815. For three years after the Peace of Vienna he had been the champion of liberalism in Europe and the competitor of Metternich for political supremacy. But from the Congress of Aix-la Chapelle in 1818 he gradually fell more and more under the influence of Metternich, and with him saw only one enemy in Europe to oppose, viz., Revo-

[1] Tennent, *History of Modern Greece*, vol. ii, chap. xviii.

lution. To combat it he had applauded Austrian intervention in Italy in 1820, and in 1822 he suggested French intervention in Spain, and now he did not hesitate to condemn the Greeks in unmeasured terms. But Russian official opinion was favorable to the Greeks, and Alexander's policy on the Greek question until his death was a vacillating one. On July 6, 1821, he instructed Strogonoff, his ambassador at Constantinople, to demand, first, that the Porte re-erect the churches destroyed by the Turkish mobs in the recent outbreaks; second, that it guarantee the protection of the Christian religion in the Ottoman Empire, and third, that it re-establish in the Danubian principalities the legal regime existing before the outbreaks, and remove the Turkish troops.[1] These demands the Porte peremptorily refused; Strogonoff left Constantinople August 8, 1821, and diplomatic relations between Russia and Turkey were severed. Alexander massed his troops along the Pruth, but he hesitated to take the initiative in hostilities. There were at least two powers in Europe which were not disposed to stand idly by and permit Russia to work her will in the Balkans. These powers were Austria and England; and Alexander, besides hesitating to incur their opposition in a contest with Turkey, did not desire to face the dissolution of the system, based on the Holy Alliance, of which he was the author and Austria the mainstay. Metternich and Castlereagh both were opposed to the Greeks, the former seeing in their revolt only another symptom of the Revolution which was raising its head all over Europe, and the latter only the possible fruition of Russian schemes. Both wrote to Alexander that this was a splendid opportunity for him to stand by his principles and give an example to Europe;[2] and as neither the French nor the Prussian government exhibited any en-

---

[1] *British and Foreign State Papers*, vol. viii, pp. 1251 *et seq*. For the Turkish reply, *ibid.*, p. 1260.

[2] Metternich's Memorandum for the Emperor Alexander, in *Metternich's Memoirs*, vol. iii, p. 611.

thusiasm in his behalf, and as on January 13, 1822, the Greek
national assembly adopted a democratic constitution and declared the complete independence of Hellas, Alexander decided
to yield.¹   He accepted the mediation of Austria and England,
who urged the Porte to grant the demands which he made on
the strength of the treaties, and especially that which concerned the Danubian principalities.   In May the Porte promised to nominate two new hospodars for Moldavia and Wallachia, and asked Russia to resume diplomatic relations.²
Alexander expressed his willingness to comply with this request, on condition that the Porte should notify him officially
of the nomination of the two hospodars, should renew the
commercial privileges of Russia in the Ottoman Empire, and
should re-establish the rights and privileges of the Christians,
the violations of which had caused the uprising of the Greeks.³
Three months later the Congress of Verona assembled, and
Alexander completed his submission to the policy of Metter-
nich.⁴   The Congress declined to admit the Greek delegation,
and condemned the revolution; and the Greek delegates, after
lingering several weeks at Ancona, were invited by the police
of the Holy See to depart.

August 12, 1822, Castlereagh committed suicide, and the
" malevolent meteor," ⁵ George Canning, soon became the
head of the foreign office in London.   Not only did Canning

---

¹ For the Greek Declaration of Independence and Constitution, see *British
Foreign and State Papers*, vol. ix, pp. 620–629.

² *British and Foreign State Papers*, vol. x, pp. 850 *et seq.*

³ *Annuaire Lesur* for 1823, p. 521.

⁴ *Metternich's Memoirs*, vol. iii, p. 523.   "In this fresh emergency the Emperor Alexander has given proof of his noble and loyal courage . . . .   The two
monarchs, *i. e.*, of Russia and Austria, have simultaneously declared at Constantinople that faithful to the principles which they have publicly announced, they
will never support the enemies of public order; that they will never lend any help
to the Greek insurgents; that they leave to the Porte itself the task of watching
over its own safety."

⁵ *Metternich's Memoirs*, vol. iii, p. 392.

take the keenest pleasure in defying Metternich openly, and ridiculing him in the eyes of Europe, but as the friend of liberalism, he was a strong partisan of the Greek cause. From the beginning of 1823 the friendly attitude of England towards the Greeks was shown in many ways. The English government of the Ionian Islands gave them passive assistance;[1] the blockade established by the Greeks at various ports along the coast was recognized by the English government,[2] which also issued a proclamation of neutrality, thus recognizing the Greeks as belligerents ; and a loan of eight hundred thousand pounds was raised in London for the Greek government. The Greeks indeed began to consider England as their only friend in Europe, and English influence naturally became predominant with them. Towards the end of 1823, Alexander, who was greatly disturbed by these developments, invited the four great powers to send delegates to a conference at St. Petersburg to consider the pacification of Greece. Canning demanded that previously to the opening of the conference, Russia should make known her views as to the reorganization of the country. In a memoir to the four courts Alexander proposed that Greece should be divided into three parts—Morea, East Hellas and West Hellas—each of which should be a vassal principality to the Porte on substantially the same basis as the Danubian principalities.[3]

The object of this was evident. The Ottoman Empire was to be dismembered, but no new state was to be founded which would be strong enough to stand by itself. On the contrary, the Greeks were to be dissevered, and were to be placed in a situation in which they would, like the Danubian principalities, be obliged to look to Russia for support. The Sultan, it is needless to say, was indignant at the proposal of a conference for the dismemberment of his empire and the settlement of the relations which

[1] *British and Foreign State Papers*, vol. xii, p. 903.

[2] Hansard's *Parliamentary Debates*, new series, vol. ix, p. 441.

[3] Menzies, *Turkey, Old and New*, p. 365.

should exist between him and rebellious subjects from whom
he demanded unconditional surrender. The Greeks, on the
other hand, who up to this time had been uniformly successful
against the Turks, were equally incensed at what they
denounced as Alexander's betrayal of them, and refused to be
divided or to become a vassal state. They turned naturally
to the power which had befriended them, and in August,
1824, addressed a note to Canning, in which they rejected the
proposals of Alexander, and besought Canning to defend their
independence.[1] In November Canning made a temperate
reply. He declared that mediation was at the time impossible
because the views of the two belligerents were so diverse, and
because England was united to Turkey by ancient treaties
which the Sultan had not violated. Meanwhile, Great Britain
would observe a strict neutrality,[2] and if at a future time
Greece should demand her mediation, and the Ottoman Porte
should accept it, it would be at their service. At the same
time Canning notified Alexander that Stratford Canning, who
had been designated as the English representative at the proposed conference at St. Petersburg, would not take part in its
deliberations, but would confine his negotiations with Russia
to the question of the boundary between the two states in
North America.[3] In reality Canning was convinced that the
conference could accomplish nothing, for he was assured both
at Constantinople and at Nauplie, the seat of the Greek government, that the collective mediation of the powers would be
rejected by both Turkey and Greece, and he was unwilling to
support any plan to compel them to accept it.

Alexander deeply resented Canning's refusal to take part in
the conference. But Canning had reasoned correctly. At the
conference, which was in session from February to April, 1825,
Russia kept to the front the plan of demanding of the belliger-

---

[1] *British Foreign and State Papers*, vol. xii, p. 899.

[2] Hertzlet's *Map of Europe by Treaty*, vol. i, p. 731.

[3] Lane Poole, *Life of Stratford Canning*, chap. x.

ents an armistice, of offering them a collective mediation, and
if they refused, of compelling them to accept. It was evidently
Alexander's design that the Holy Alliance should perform in
the Balkans a duty similar to that which it had discharged in
Italy and Spain, and that on the present occasion Russia should
be delegated to execute the task. But the other members of
the Holy Alliance also had their individual interests to consult.
France feared to lose her influence with Mehemet Ali, who had
been called by Mahmoud from Egypt to take part in the Greek
struggle. Austria would never agree that Russia should lead
an army through the Balkans, and Prussia would not go
counter to anything suggested by Metternich. At length
Metternich took a definite stand. He refused any compromise.
There must be on the part of the Greeks either entire submission or entire independence; and he knew that Alexander
would not agree to the latter.[1] The result of the long sessions
of the conference was that the powers engaged to ask the Porte
to grant the just demands of its subjects, and in case of refusal, to offer it their mediation.

The ingratitude of Austria, as Alexander considered it,
impelled him to approach Canning, and this inclination was
strengthened by the reply given at Constantinople to the note
of the conference. The Sultan declared that he would confirm
his revolted subjects in their privileges and guarantees after
they had unconditionally surrendered, and that in the mean
time he would not recognize the intervention either of one
power or of a group of powers. Ibrahim Pasha, the son of
Mehemet Ali, who had been sent by the latter to command
the Ottoman forces, had turned the tide of war in Greece, and
the Sultan looked for a speedy termination of the struggle, as
in fact did all Europe, unless the powers should soon intervene.
But from the moment of the Sultan's reply, the attitude of
Russia towards Turkey resumed all its old severity. The Czar
renewed his complaints at the non-performance of the promises

---

[1] Metternich to Lebzelten, in *Metternich's Memoirs*, vol. iv, p. 209.

of the Porte. He demanded that the last of the Turkish troops should be removed from the principalities, that the liberties guaranteed to the Serbs by the Treaty of Bucharest should be conceded to them, and that their deputies to Constantinople, who had been imprisoned since the revolt began, in 1821, should be released. These demands were emphasized by increasing the Russian forces along the Pruth. August 25, 1825, the Greeks once more voted to place themselves under the protection of England, and so notified Canning.[1] The latter answered, that while England could not at that moment accede to their wishes, she would, nevertheless, watch over them and not permit any other power to impose a solution contrary to their interests. Strangely enough, it was with the full knowledge of this answer, which evidently was leveled at Russia, that Alexander began his approach to England. But on December 1, 1825, before anything could be accomplished, he died.

His successor, Nicholas, on ascending the throne declared that it was his purpose to follow the plans of Alexander, and that, as the latter had intended to compel the Porte to accede to his demands, it therefore behooved him to continue in that path.[2] On April 5, 1826, he accordingly addressed to the Porte an ultimatum, in which he demanded that the Sultan, besides restoring the Danubian principalities to their position previous to the insurrection of 1821, and fulfilling the stipulations of the Treaty of Bucharest, should send commissioners to the frontier to negotiate with Russian commissioners concerning the disputes arising out of that treaty.[3] Six weeks were allowed to the Porte to yield. Nothing was said in the ultimatum as to the fate of the Greeks, but Nicholas frequently

---

[1] *British and Foreign State Papers*, vol. xii, p. 904.

[2] See his interview with Count Zicky, the Austrian envoy, *Metternich's Memoirs*, vol. iv, p. 486.

[3] For the full text of the ultimatum, see *British and Foreign State Papers*, vol. xiii, p. 1056.

spoke of them as rebels who deserved no help in their revolt against their sovereign.[1]   Canning resolved to prevent a rupture between Russia and Turkey by all means.   A victorious Russian army in Turkey would mean that Nicholas would lay down the law for the entire Balkan peninsula, and settle the Greek question to suit himself.   This Canning determined to prevent.   He therefore sent the Duke of Wellington, for whom Nicholas had a great admiration, on a mission to St. Petersburg, ostensibly to congratulate the Czar on his accession to the throne, but in reality to come to terms on the Eastern question.   Wellington was to tender the good offices of England in the disputes between Russia and Turkey, and to request Nicholas' adhesion to the British mediation between the Greeks and the Turks.   Nicholas flatly refused any interference between himself and the Porte in what concerned his particular grievances; but Wellington made it clear to him that England could remain neutral in a war between Russia and Turkey only in case he should agree to British mediation between the Greeks and the Turks; and Nicholas, disclaiming any particular interest in the fate of the rebels, signed the protocol of April 4, 1826.[2]   By this protocol it was provided that Russia should accept the mediation of Great Britain between the Greeks and the Turks; that autonomy should be demanded for Greece, but that she should remain tributary to the Porte; that the agreement should hold good whatever might be the relations between Russia and Turkey; that each of the contracting parties should renounce in advance all advantages which would not be common to all the states of Europe as a

---

[1] See the Zicky interview, *Metternich's Memoirs*, vol, iv, p. 489.   "I repeat that I detest and abhor the Greeks, although they are my co-religionists; they have behaved in a shocking, blamable and even criminal manner.   I look upon them as subjects in revolt against their legitimate sovereign.   I do not desire their enfranchisement.   They do not deserve it; and it would be a very bad example for all other countries if they succeeded in establishing it."

[2] Hertslet's *Map of Europe by Treaty*, vol. i, p. 741.

consequence of the definitive pacification of Greece ; and finally, that a guarantee of the future state of things should be solicited of all the great powers of Europe.

Canning at the same time sent Stratford Canning to the Levant to make known to both the Greeks and the Turks the plan of pacification which was desired by Great Britain. This plan, conformably to the Tory policy of preserving the integrity of the Ottoman Empire, did not contemplate the erection of a new free maritime state, but merely proposed that Greece, while receiving a grant of autonomy, should remain tributary to the Porte. Nevertheless, it was gladly accepted by the Greeks, who were now driven to their last extremity ; but, when Stratford Canning reached Constantinople, he was received by the Sultan with reproaches.[1] The Divan was encouraged by Austria to resist the English plan. Metternich, who desired above all things to prevent a war in the Balkans, which might spread to central Europe, advised the Porte to yield to the demands of the Czar's ultimatum, but to reject the British proposal of compromise with the rebels. The Porte followed this advice. The Reis Effendi again declared to Stratford Canning that the Sultan would never admit the intervention of a third party between himself and his rebellious subjects, but on May 12, 1826, notified the Russian chargé d'affaires that the Sultan accepted the proposals of the Czar. The last Turkish troops were withdrawn from the principalities; the Servian deputies were released; and two negotiators were sent to meet the representatives of the Czar in Bessarabia. Mahmoud was all the more willing to agree to the Russian ultimatum, since he had just destroyed the Janissaries and had not had time to form a new army on the European basis, so that in case of war he would have been at the mercy of the Czar. October 7, 1827, there was signed the Treaty of Ackerman.[2] The Treaty of Bucharest was ex-

[1] *Annuaire Lesur* for 1826, p. 375.

[2] Hertslet's *Map of Europe by Treaty*, vol. i, p. 747.

pressly confirmed. The privileges of Moldavia and Wallachia were assured by a renewal of the Hatti-sheriff of 1802; Servia was to receive the constitution which had been so long delayed; the Czar was to retain all the places in Asia that were in his possession; the Ottoman Porte was to recompense Russian subjects for all losses due to the Barbary pirates; finally, the Russians were to enjoy in all Ottoman seas and ports full liberty of commerce. Two annexed conventions related to the principalities and Servia respectively. The first provided that the hospodars should be elected for seven years from the native Boyards with the approval of the Ottoman Porte, and that they should not be removed except with the consent of the Czar; that taxes should be regulated by the authorities of the country, and that a remission of two years' tribute should be accorded. The second additional convention provided that the Porte and the Servian deputies should agree on measures to secure to Servia liberty of worship, the choice of local rulers, the consolidation of the different taxes into one, and liberty of commerce.

Meanwhile, the protocol of April 4, as agreed to by Wellington and Nicholas, had been officially communicated to the other great powers. Austria promptly rejected it. True to the principles of the Holy Alliance, Metternich declared that the only proper pacification would be for the Sultan freely to grant the desired privileges.[1] At Metternich's dictation the protocol was also rejected at Berlin. But it received different treatment at Paris. Nicholas urged the French government to accede to it in order to checkmate British influence in Greece. Canning urged it with equal energy in order to counterbalance Russia in the Balkan Peninsula. The French government, anxious to recover its lost prestige in the East, not only accepted it, but demanded that it be converted into a formal alliance between France, England and Russia for the

[1] The Austrian answer to the protocol of April 4th is given in *Metternich's Memoirs*, vol. iv, p. 339.

pacification of the Levant. This was agreed to in principle
by the three powers in January, 1827, and there remained
for discussion only the details for the common execution of the
project. In February the protocol of April 4 was communicated to the Porte, but the Turkish ministers, encouraged by
the sinister policy of Metternich, who urged delay until Ibrahim should complete his conquest of the Morea, deferred their
answer till Athens was taken in June, and then curtly replied
that the Sultan would repel all interference of another state in
his relations with his subjects.[1] The almost immediate result
of this refusal was the signing of the Treaty of London of July
7, 1827, between England, France and Russia.[2] The preamble
recited that the allied powers were impelled by the necessity
of putting an end to a condition of affairs so disastrous to their
commerce, by humanity and by the appeals of the Greek
government to two of them, France and England. The
general conditions of the treaty were the same as those of the
protocol of April 4; but for its execution an additional article
was added which provided that the collective mediation of the
three powers should be offered to the Porte in a note; that, if
the offer was refused, the Porte should, after not more than a
month's delay, be notified in a second note that the allies
would accredit consuls to the principal cities of Greece and
receive consuls from them, and would impose an armistice by
force of arms if necessary upon the two belligerents, it being
understood that by so doing they did not intend to place
themselves in a state of war with either belligerent.

In the beginning of August, 1827, the Greek government
was notified of the Treaty of London and hastened to accept
it, but the Ottoman Porte summarily rejected it. On August
30th notice was given to the Porte that the allies intended to
begin coercive measures, but it still refused to grant any concession. The allies then proceeded to the preliminaries of

[1] *British and Foreign State Papers*, vol. xiv, p. 1042.
[2] Hertslet's *Map of Europe by Treaty*, vol. i, p. 769.

execution, and their ambassadors at Constantinople ordered the admirals of the three fleets to prevent all transport or employment of Ottoman forces on the coast of what would probably be the new Greek state.[1]　On the other hand, the Greek forces were ordered to remove themselves from all place soutside its limits.　In conformity with their orders the allied fleets under Admiral Codrington entered the Bay of Navarino October 20, 1827, and notified Ibrahim to quit Greece.[2]　A conflict ensued, in which the Turco-Egyptian fleet was destroyed; and Ibrahim agreed to cease hostilities against the Greeks.　The news of Navarino produced different effects upon the two belligerents.　The Greeks naturally were overjoyed, and no longer having to fear the enemy, became very active, extending their operations beyond the boundaries allotted to them, in the hope that the great powers would accept accomplished facts.　Sultan Mahmoud, on the contrary, was infuriated, and was less disposed than ever to treat with his revolted subjects, or to submit to the mediation of the powers which had now destroyed his fleet; and he demanded of the three powers an open disavowal of and a full indemnity for the outrage which had been committed.　This was refused by the ambassadors of those powers November 10th,[3] and for the next month they vainly endeavored to induce the Sultan to agree to the conditions of the treaty of London.　All they could obtain was a promise that if the Greeks would as revolted subjects unconditionally submit, he would grant an armistice, restore the condition of things existing in Greece previous to 1821, and give to the country an administration which should be both mild and just.　In despair, the ambassadors of the three powers demanded their passports, and quitted Constantinople December 8, 1827.

[1] Instruction addressed to the Admirals, *British and Foreign State Papers*, vol. xvii, p. 20.

[2] This is shown by the protocol of the admirals drawn up previously to their entrance in Navarino, *British and Foreign State Papers*, vol. xiv, p. 1050.

[3] *British and Foreign State Papers*. vol. xv, p. 1103.

Immediately there began all over Turkey a massacre of
Christians, especially of Russians, and on December 20th
Mahmoud called together the ayans, or heads of the Mussulman districts, and issued to them a violent manifesto,[1] accus-
ing Russia of having incessantly incited revolt in his dominions since 1821, and of having cheated him at Ackerman,
where her envoys had promised no longer to interfere in the
Greek question.   He added that the time had come to uphold
the honor of outraged Islam, and he appealed to the faithful
for support.   Nicholas resolved not to allow Mahmoud to
outstrip him.   On January 6, 1828, he proposed to the allies
a plan of coercion much more drastic than that already
adopted.[2]   The principalities were to be occupied by Russian
troops; the allied fleets were to blockade Alexandria and
Constantinople so as to deliver and defend the Morea; and
the allies were to support Capodistrias, the president of the
Greek state, by supplying him with money; while they were
also to order their ambassadors, who had left Constantinople,
to assemble at Corfu to confer on means of pacification.   In
the meantime, on August 8, 1827, George Canning had died.
He was succeeded by the Duke of Wellington, at the head of
a ministry of Old Tories, who, in accordance with their traditional policy, discountenanced all measures looking to Greek
independence.   For the definite and strenuous system of
Canning, the new cabinet substituted tentative and desultory
expedients intended to oppose and neutralize the influence of
Russia.   It turned to France, but France, besides being Phil-
Hellene, wished to take some action, which, while serving to
check the Czar, would also increase her own prestige.   She
therefore asked to be deputed to send an army of occupation
into the Morea.   This was not pleasing to the Wellington
ministry, but as it was averse to assuming itself a directly

[1] *British and Foreign State Papers*, vol. xiv, p. 1052.

[2] Count Nesselrode to Prince Lieven, *British and Foreign State Papers*, vol.
xvii, p. 30.

hostile attitude toward Turkey, and desired to establish a counterpoise to the Czar, it reluctantly yielded to the French proposal.[1]

At the end of February, Nicholas notified the powers that he considered Mahmoud's manifesto of December 20th as equivalent to a declaration of war, and that he was determined to answer it by force; that he would be glad to carry out the terms of the Treaty of London in union with his allies, but that he must, in any event, obtain redress for his own particular grievances.[2]   The Wellington cabinet, disappointed by its failure to obtain the full co-operation of France against the Czar, made a virtue of necessity, and, in order to prevent any independent action on his part in the Mediterranean, demanded that the allied fleets should operate only in conformity with the Treaty of London and the collective decisions of the contracting parties.[3] Nicholas agreed to this and to the French occupation of the Morea, and on April 26, 1828, declared war against Turkey.[4] On July 2d, the conferences of the allies were resumed at London, and on August 7th, the three ambassadors assembled at Corfu to concert a plan for the pacification of Greece. The Sultan, after the Russians had occupied the principalities, assumed a more moderate position, and hoping to disrupt the triple alliance, invited France and England to send back their ambassadors to treat on the Greek question at Constantinople. Wellington, however, fearing if that were done Nicholas would consider himself absolved from the engagements of the Treaty of London and would, at the head of a victorious army, overthrow the entire established order in

[1] The proposal and agreement may be seen in *British and Foreign State Papers*, vol xvi, p. 1083; also in *Parliamentary Debates*, Hansard's, new series, vol. xxii, pp. 345 et seq.

[2] *British and Foreign State Papers*, vol. xvii, p. 50.

[3] The Earl of Aberdeen to Prince Lieven, *British and Foreign State Papers*, vol. xvii, p. 114.

[4] Hertslet's *Map of Europe by Treaty*, vol. ii, p. 777.

the East, rejected the proposal; and the alliance was maintained.[1]

The campaign of 1828 proved disastrous to the Russians, much to the joy of Metternich,[2] who encouraged the Turks and sounded the other courts as to a coalition against Russia. This suggestion was everywhere rejected.[3] But Wellington, encouraged by the Russian reverses, prevailed upon France to agree to a protocol, November 16, 1828, by which it was agreed that the two powers should send their ambassadors to Constantinople to urge upon the Porte the necessity of pacification; but the protocol was accepted by France only on condition that it should not be carried into effect unless Nicholas should acquiesce in it. The Czar gave his consent with the proviso that, before the British and French ambassadors should proceed to Constantinople, the London conference should adopt a definite plan of pacification. Such a plan was adopted, March 22, 1829.[4] By its principal clauses, which had been agreed to by Capodistrias and the ambassadors at Corfu,[5] the new Greek state was to include the Morea, the Cyclades and continental Greece as far as the Gulfs of Orta and Volo. This state was to have a monarchical government with a Christian prince, who was to be selected by the three powers and approved by the Porte, but was not to be a member of the reigning family of any of the three allies; and it was to pay an annual tribute to the Porte of one million five hundred thousand piastres and recompense Ottoman proprietors, who were

[1] *British and Foreign State Papers*, vol. xvii, p. 91.

[2] The work of Prokesch-Osten, *Geschichte des Abfalls der Griechen vom Osmanischen Reiche*, is largely devoted to defending the attitude of Metternich during the Greek Revolution. The last four volumes are valuable for the collection of documents relating to the Revolution.

[3] For an excellent description of the diplomatic aspect of Europe at the time, see dispatch of Count Pozzo di Borgo to Count Nesselrode in Martens, *Nouveau Supplément aux Recueil des Traités*, vol. iii, p. 347.

[4] Hertslet's *Map of Europe by Treaty*, vol. ii, p. 804.

[5] *Ibid.*, vol. ii, p. 798.

to be required to leave Greece. The Turkish government received the French and English ambassadors with respect, but refused to accept the new plan.[1] It was evident that the Porte would yield only to superior force.

The campaign of 1829 proved to be decisive. Diebitsch made his extraordinary march across the Balkans and appeared before Adrianople August 20th. As long as the Russians were at a distance, Mahmoud was unyielding; but now all Constantinople was in terror. The Prussian agent, de Royer, was sent in haste to conclude a peace in the name of Turkey, and it was by his mediation that there was signed, September 14, 1829, the Peace of Adrianople.[2] By this treaty the Czar restored to Turkey all his conquests in Europe except the islands at the mouth of the Danube, but retained most of the cities and fortresses taken in Asia. All the rights and privileges of Moldavia, Wallachia and Servia were confirmed and guaranteed. The free navigation of the Dardanelles and Bosporous was secured to the ships of all powers with whom the Porte was at peace. Russian subjects were to have full liberty of commerce in the entire Ottoman Empire. The Sultan was to reimburse the Czar for the full expenses of the war, and satisfy his particular grievances to the extent of eleven and a half millions of Dutch ducats (137,000,000 francs), as a guarantee of which Moldavia, Wallachia and Bulgaria were to remain in the occupation of the Russians. Finally, the Ottoman Porte agreed, purely and simply, in all that concerned Greece, to the Treaty of London of July 6, 1827, and the protocol of March 22, 1829. Two supplementary conventions were added to the treaty of peace—one relative to the payment of the indemnity, the other to the status of Moldavia and Wallachia. The latter introduced an innovation to the effect that the hospodars should be appointed for life, instead of for seven years, and that the fortresses be-

[1] See *Annuaire Lesur* for 1829, p. 419.

[2] Hertslet's *Map of Europe by Treaty*, vol. ii, p. 813.

longing to Turkey on the left bank of the Danube should be
dismantled. The Treaty of Adrianople was undoubtedly a
brilliant triumph for Russian policy. By the autonomy
granted to Moldavia, Wallachia, Servia and Greece, all of
whom felt that they owed their privileges to Russia, and all of
whom were subject to her domination, and by the indemnities
which the Sultan was unable to pay, the Ottoman Empire
was exposed on all sides to Russian intrigue, and was placed
at the mercy of the Czar.

The Turkish government proceeded to carry out the stipulations of the treaty, endeavoring to evade only those that
related to the Greek question, and to the payment of the
indemnities. On the latter point it obtained a substantial concession. After a long negotiation the Czar reduced the
indemnity by three millions of ducats, and evacuated all territory south of the Danube. He knew that it would be a long
while before Turkey could free herself from the debts, and in
consequence of the destruction of the fortresses in the principalities, the Russians could reach the Balkans at will. Moreover, in return for this concession, the Sultan yielded his
objections to the arrangement concerning Greece.[1] The
Greek government, however, protested vigorously against any
form of vassalage to Turkey, and in so doing was supported
by France, and strangely enough, still more by England.
The British government felt that it would not do to subject
Greece to a regime similar to that of the principalities, where
Russia could provoke new conflicts and create occasions for
intervention at will. The London conference, which had resumed its labors in October, 1829, decided, therefore, that no
tie should bind Greece to Turkey.[2] Russia did not object,
since she expected that, as the result of recent events, her
influence in Greece would be preserved; but in order still

[1] Hertslet's *Map of Europe by Treaty*, vol. 2, p. 812.

[2] The protocol of Feb. 3d, 1830, in Hertslet's *Map of Europe by Treaty*, vol.
ii, p. 841.

further to enfeeble Turkey, and at the same time to create vexations for England in the possession of the Ionian Islands, she proposed to extend the boundaries of Greece. This England refused to do. The provisions of the protocol of March 22nd were carried out, and Greece was launched as a full-fledged state. But the Greek Revolution had not resulted in merely bringing forth a new state and making a rent in the Ottoman Empire. It had also disrupted the Holy Alliance, having set two members of it, France and Russia, against the other two members, Austria and Prussia.[1]

[1] Metternich to the Emperor Francis, October 9th, 1829, in *Metternich's Memoirs*, vol. iv, p. 635.

CHAPTER V

THE EGYPTIAN REBELLION.

DESPITE the disasters of the recent war, disasters which his subjects laid wholly to the western innovations that he had introduced, Sultan Mahmoud continued with his reforms. Whether he could have successfully carried them out is more than doubtful, but his energies were soon diverted to another object.[1] The rebellions which broke out in Albania and Bosnia he quickly suppressed;[2] but he soon came into conflict, though not on account of reforms, with one of his subjects whom he found to be stronger than himself. This subject was Mehemet Ali, pasha of Egypt. Mehemet had quickly recovered from the catastrophe at Navarino, had formed a splendid army, officered principally by Frenchmen, had rebuilt his fleet and had acquired a full treasury, the result of taxes wrung from his subjects, whom he governed as a despot, but to whom he gave peace. Mehemet, as a reward for his services in the Morea, had received the pashalik of Crete; but he felt ill repaid for his exertions, and decided to seek compensation in Syria. Conscious of his strength, he resolved to enlarge the boundaries of Egypt, and also to make the possession of it hereditary in his family. The governor of Syria at this time was Abdallah Pasha, his personal enemy, who gave a refuge to all Egyptians who fled from Mehemet's despotism. An excuse for a conflict, therefore, was not wanting, when, early in 1832, a war broke out between these two servants of the Sul-

[1] For a description of Mahmoud and his reforms, see *Von Moltke's Gesammelte Schriften*, vol. viii, particularly Letter 66, p. 428.

[2] *Annuaire Lesur*, 1830, p. 669.

tan. Mahmoud ordered Mehemet to cease hostilities and to submit the quarrel to him, but Mehemet paid no attention to his commands. His adopted son, Ibrahim, a man of great ability, soon overran the whole of Syria; and on May 27, 1832, St. Jean d'Acre, the key to the country, fell into the hands of Ibrahim. Mahmoud proclaimed Mehemet an outlaw, but Ibrahim continued on his victorious career, successively defeating the three armies sent against him by the Sultan. He then crossed the Taurus, overran Asia Minor, and began his march towards Constantinople, always protesting that it was not his intention to overthrow the dynasty of the Osmanlis, but to consolidate it. Mahmoud, whose last army had been destroyed, turned to the European powers for help.[1]

The diplomatic situation in Europe at this time was peculiar. Nicholas, who had been very friendly to France under the Restoration, was decidedly inimical to the July Monarchy and thwarted it at every opportunity, though he had been unable actively to show his hostility since 1830 because of the Polish rebellion. The reactionary powers, Austria and Prussia, were also unfriendly to Louis Philippe, the "King of the Barricades," but were well disposed towards Russia for maintaining the principles of the Holy Alliance. To establish an equilibrium against these three powers in favor of Liberalism, England had formed an *entente cordiale* with the July Monarchy, but the two governments soon grew mutually distrustful, and frequently worked at cross purposes.[2] On the Eastern question, which had once more come up for settlement, each power took its stand according to its interests. With England, and especially with Palmerston, who controlled her foreign affairs during a great part of this period, the maintenance of the integrity of the Ottoman Empire was a dogma,[3] and Palmerston looked upon Mehemet as a menace to that

[1] *Annual Register*, 1832, pp. 400 *et seq.*

[2] This is evident in the memoirs of statesmen of the period.

[3] Bulwer's *Life of Palmerston*, vol. iii, book 12 *passim.*

integrity.[1] But the attention of Englishmen was engrossed with home affairs in 1832, and the great desire of the government with reference to the Eastern question was that it might be promptly closed, before Russia could take advantage of the situation. Nicholas, on the other hand, was the most pronounced enemy the Ottoman Empire then had, but, strangely enough, he determined to oppose Mehemet in the belief that the latter would prove to be its regenerator, and postpone indefinitely the success of Russian designs. Austria, who feared Russian ascendancy in the Balkans, supported the English position, looking upon Mehemet as a rebel against legitimate authority, and upholding the Sultan against his vassal.[2] Only France supported Mehemet. The Pasha of Egypt was looked upon by Frenchmen as a sort of client of France. His army and civil service were officered principally by Frenchmen, and French influence in Egypt predominated over that of any other power. Frenchmen would not have forgiven the July Monarchy had it abandoned Mehemet. But it was, besides, a rule of French foreign policy to maintain the integrity of the Ottoman Empire against Russian aggression, and it was doubly so now, when Russia was unfriendly. And the supporters of the July Monarchy believed that the best way to uphold the sovereignty of Turkey against Russian designs was to make of Egypt a strong rear guard. Louis Philippe, however, did not venture to support Mehemet openly, because of England's jealousy of French influence in Egypt; and the thing most necessary to Louis Philippe at this time was the English alliance. So the July Monarchy adopted a policy which was not only deceitful, but which also eventually brought it into discredit and danger.[3]

Mahmoud naturally turned first to those powers whom he

[1] *British and Foreign State Papers*, vol. xxvi, p. 269, no. 4.

[2] *Aus Metternich's Nachgelassenen Papieren*, vol. v, no. 1128.

[3] For the position of the various powers as to Mehemet Ali, see *Debidour, Histoire Diplomatique*, vol. i, chap. 9.

considered friendly and requested their assistance.[1]   England, however, was too much engrossed in home affairs to take an active part in settling the new complications.[2]   M. de Varennes, the French chargé d'affaires, tendered his good offices to the Ottoman Porte, and when they were accepted, he requested Ibrahim, in the name of France, not to continue his march, and advised Mehemet to accept the southern half of Syria, Unfortunately, France had as consul-general at Alexandria. M. Mimaut, who was devoted to the interests of Mehemet and who professed to believe that the advice of de Verennes was designed to meet diplomatic exigencies and was not to be taken seriously.   He therefore counseled Mehemet to refuse it.   This course was taken, and Ibrahim resumed his march and encamped within a few miles of Scutari.   Mahmoud, in terror, immediately invoked, January 31, 1833, the assistance of the Russian fleet, and on the 20th of February it anchored under the palace of the Sultan.   At this moment Admiral Roussin, the French ambassador, arrived.   Roussin was a fiery old soldier, who was very zealous for his country's honor, and to whom the Russian flag was hateful.   He demanded that the Russian fleet be sent away at once.   Mahmoud answered that he would gladly accede to his request if he would persuade Mehemet to agree to the terms recommended by de Varennes.   Roussin took it upon himself to see that this should be done.   But Mehemet, who was still acting upon the counsels of Mimaut, rejected the terms again, and demanded not only the whole of Syria, but also the district of Adana, the possession of which would open to him the whole of Asia Minor ; and he ordered Ibrahim to recommence operations.[3]

[1] *British and Foreign State Papers*, vol. xxii, p. 140 *et seq.*

[2] The reform bill excitement was prevalent. See Hansard's *Parliamentary Debates*, third series, vol. xix, p. 578, for Palmerston's admission that England had refused assistance to the Ottoman Porte.

[3] *Annual Register*, 1833, p. 288.

The result of Roussin's negotiations was that Mahmoud, instead of sending away the Russian fleet, asked, March 20, 1833, that it be reinforced by a Russian army. Fifteen days later twelve thousand Russian troops encamped at Scutari, and a Russian army began to form in the Danubian principalities. Both England and Austria now became alarmed and ordered their ambassadors at Constantinople to support the French proposals; and the ambassadors of the three powers made upon Mahmoud an energetic demand that he come to terms with Mehemet, at whatever sacrifice might be necessary, so as to do away with the need of Russian assistance. Nor was Russia greatly opposed to the Porte's yielding to the demands of Mehemet; for Nicholas had now discovered that the aim of Mehemet was territorial aggrandizement and not the regeneration of the Ottoman Empire. The more the Sultan was enfeebled the more he would need the assistance of the Czar. Mahmoud therefore succumbed, and on May 1st issued a Hatti-sheriff relieving Mehemet from his outlawry and conceding everything that he required.[1]

Russia no longer had any pretext for occupying the Bosphorus, and when asked to remove her troops and fleet, she did so, July 10, 1833. But it soon transpired that for her prompt compliance there was a special cause. On July 8th, only two days previously, she had concluded with the Sultan the Treaty of Unkiar Skelessi, which practically made Turkey a feudatory of the Czar.[2] It bound the two powers to a defensive alliance for eight years against all others, each placing itself at the disposal of the other for defense against both external and internal dangers. Considering the internal disorders which constantly disturbed the Ottoman Empire, and the ease with which the Czar could foment such disorders, the alliance held out to Nicholas untold possibilities of intervention in Ottoman affairs. He took good care, however, to guard against these possibili-

[1] *Annuaire Lesur*, 1833, p. 445 *et seq.*

[2] Hertslet's *Map of Europe by Treaty*, vol. ii, p. 925.

ties becoming reciprocal. By a separate article it was provided that, in case the Czar should stand in need of the assistance of his ally, the latter should be excused from furnishing active aid, but should be considered as fulfilling all his engagements by simply closing the Dardanelles to the enemies of the Czar. This would make Russia practically invulnerable to the states from which she had most to fear. An attack from either France or England by way of the Mediterranean would then be impossible. They could not cross Germany, and the Baltic admitted of active operations for but a few months in the year. The French and English governments were greatly exercised, and demanded explanations of both St. Petersburg and Constantinople. The explanations which they obtained were very unsatisfactory,[1] and both governments sent powerful fleets to the Aegean. For a time a war with Russia seemed to be probable, but the excitement, after venting itself in vigorous protests, soon subsided.

Though Sultan Mahmoud yielded to his vassal in 1833, he cherished an intention to recover his lost provinces, and the events of the year following the settlement tended to disturb his peaceful relations with Mehemet. The latter's attempt to establish stable government among the wild tribes of Syria was constantly thwarted by the revolts which Mahmoud secretly instigated. And Mehemet made no secret of his intention to found a dynasty and transmit to his heirs the possession of his dominions.[2] In conformity with this design he withheld payment of the tribute due to his sovereign; and their relations became more and more strained till an open conflict took place early in 1839. The Turkish army, which Mahmoud had been gathering for some years, crossed the Euphrates April 21st. This event naturally increased the anxiety which the powers had already exhibited with regard

[1] Hertslet's *Map of Europe by Treaty*, vol. ii, p. 428.

[2] See his notification to the French and English consuls general, May 25th, 1838, in *British and Foreign State Papers*, vol. 26, p. 696.

to the situation.[1] The eight years during which the Treaty of Unkiar Skelessi was to last had not yet expired, and under its provisions Russia could send an army to Constantinople.[2] Palmerston made approaches to Louis Philippe, who was glad to act in accord with him in order to strengthen the English alliance, which showed signs of weakness. The two governments sent fleets to the Aegean, with instructions to force the Dardanelles if the Russian fleet should enter the Bosphorus. In May, Metternich revived his old plan of a European conference at Vienna, but France and Russia objected to it. France was anxious to prevent the Russian occupation of the Bosphorus, but she was equally anxious that her protégé, Mehemet Ali, should not be interfered with, and she feared that if a conference should be convoked it would not confine itself to the question of the Straits. Nicholas, on the other hand, although he would have been glad to strike a blow at the July Monarchy through Mehemet Ali, declined Metternich's proposal because he knew that the question of the Straits would be the most important one to be considered.

Such was the condition of affairs when the startling news reached the European courts that on June 24, 1839, Ibrahim had routed the Turkish army, that a week later Sultan Mahmoud had died, and that immediately afterwards the Capudan Pasha with the entire Turkish fleet had gone over to Mehemet. The Ottoman Porte was now without either army or navy, and the assistance of a great power was absolutely necessary to its safety. The Divan, stricken with consternation, was about to yield unconditionally to Mehemet's demand for the hereditary possession of all his dominions, when a note was received from the powers. This note, which bears date July 27, 1839, informed the Porte that the five great powers—

---

[1] *British and Foreign State Papers*, vol. xxvi, p. 694 *et seq.*

[2] As to the anxiety caused by the Treaty of Unkiar Skelessi before the trouble of 1839, see Palmerston's letter to Ponsonby, Bulwer, *Life of Palmerston*, vol. ii, p. 247.

Austria, England, France, Prussia, and Russia—had agreed to act in concert on the Eastern question, and requested the Turkish government not to come to any definite conclusion without their advice.[1]   The Porte replied that it would await the action of Europe, and gratefully accepted the proffered mediation.   But the five great powers were not in accord as to the terms of settlement, and the divergence of views was especially wide between France and England.   Palmerston, determined to keep the Ottoman Empire intact, suggested in August, 1839, that all the provinces which Mehemet had sought to annex to Egypt be restored to their former condition, and that if Mehemet refused he should be coerced into submission.   But France, on whose co-operation Palmerston had at first counted, rejected his proposal.   Not only would she not accept it, but she made Mehemet's cause her own, and demanded for him the hereditary possession of Egypt and of all the provinces which he had conquered.   The correspondence between the two governments became daily more bitter, the people and the newspapers more and more hostile, and the alliance which had maintained the peace of Europe since 1830 appeared to be on the verge of disruption.

Nicholas regarded with grim satisfaction the clash between France and England, and determined to seize the opportunity to humiliate the July Monarchy, and to isolate France from the European concert.   On September 15th Baron Brunnow arrived at London with a plan of co-operation from the Czar.[2] The latter was ready to ally himself with the other powers in the settlement of the Eastern question,[3] and to that end was willing to renounce the Treaty of Unkiar Skelessi, but he preferred that France should be excluded from participation in the settlement.[4]   France in the mean time continued to main-

---

[1] *British and Foreign State Papers*, vol. xxviii, p. 408.

[2] For the contents of plan, see *Annuaire Lesur*, 1840, p. 442.

[3] See Bulwer, *Life of Palmerston*, vol. ii, p. 262.

[4] Seignobos, *Political History of Europe since 1814*, chap. xxvi, p. 774.

tain the position which she had taken. Thiers, the avowed
champion of French honor, became president of the council,
and ordered Guizot, then French ambassador at London, to
uphold more energetically than ever the French position.
Though Thiers did not formally withdraw the adhesion of the
French government to the note of July 27, 1839, everybody
knew that he disapproved of it,[1] and the French nation
enthusiastically supported him in his resolution to protect its
protégé. The English Cabinet, assured of Russian support,
early in 1840 invited the powers to send representatives to a
conference at London. The conference opened early in April.
Guizot played an important part in it, but his design was not
to accelerate a settlement, but to retard it. He was instructed
by Thiers to stave off a final decision until the negotiations
which had been secretly opened at Constantinople between
the Sultan and Mehemet, under the auspices of the French
ambassador, and which were expected to terminate favorably
to Mehemet, should have been concluded.[2] Unfortunately,
Thiers' scheme was well known to Palmerston, and the success of the negotiation at Constantinople was rendered null by
the activities of Ponsonby, the British ambassador.[3] After
two months of fruitless discussion at London, on January 1st
Palmerston offered to France terms of settlement which were
to be final. These were to concede to Mehemet the hereditary
dominion of Egypt, and the life possession of the pashalik of
Acre. Palmerston demanded a categorical reply, but was
answered with new dilatory measures.[4]

Palmerston now entered upon negotiations with the other

[1] Guizot, *Embassy to the Court of St. James*, chap. ii, p. 59.

[2] Guizot, *Embassy to the Court of St. James in 1840*, chap. ii, p. 60.

[3] French writers are almost unanimous on the anti-French attitude of Ponsonby
at Constantinople. The charge was also made against him in Parliament. Hansard, *Parliamentary Debates*, vol. lxi, p. 627.

[4] For the attitude of the French government on this settlement, see Guizot's
Embassy to the Court of St. James in 1840, chap. v, pp. 188 *et seq.*

three powers for a settlement of the eastern question without France, and if necessary against France. He was already assured of Russia's co-operation, and the concurrence of Austria and Prussia was also practically assured as the result of the refusal of the French government to accept terms of settlement which they had themselves suggested.[1]   Palmerston had more difficulty in persuading some of his colleagues in the British cabinet, who feared a collision with France;[2] but he convinced them that Louis Philippe would avoid war at any cost,[3] and that Mehemet would yield without conflict.   On July 15, 1840, a treaty was concluded at London between Great Britain, Russia, Austria, Prussia, and the Sultan.   It declared that the four powers first named, " animated by the desire of maintaining the integrity and independence of the Ottoman Empire as a security for the peace of Europe," would compel Mehemet Ali, if necessary by force, to accept the conditions which the Sultan had agreed to grant him; and it placed under their collective safeguard the Bosphorus and the Dardanelles and Constantinople itself.   The conditions agreed upon were to be notified to Mehemet by the Sultan, who was to offer him the hereditary administration of Egypt and the life administration of the pashalik of Acre, provided that he accepted within ten days, and at the same time ordered the withdrawal of his forces from Crete, the Holy Cities, Adana, and the northern part of Syria.   Should he fail to accept within that time, the offer of the Sultan was to be reduced to the hereditary governorship of Egypt; and in case Mehemet should not within another ten days accept this con-

---

[1] For the plan suggested by Prussia and Austria to France, see Guizot's *Embassy to the Court of St. James in 1840*, chap. ii, p. 74 *et seq.*

[2] The British Cabinet was very divided as to the wisdom of supporting Palmerston on the Eastern question.   See his letter to Melbourne in Bulwer, *Life of Palmerston*, vol. ii, p. 309; Galso uizot, *Embassy to the Court of St. James*, chap. v, p. 180.

[3] Letter to Granville at Paris in Bulwer, *Life of Palmerston*, vol. ii, p. 269.

cession, the Sultan was to be bound by nothing. Finally, contrary to diplomatic usage, it was agreed in an additional protocol that the powers should proceed to carry out the treaty without awaiting the exchange of ratifications.[1]

The treaty of the 15th of July was signed without Guizot's knowledge, and even when two days later Palmerston informed him of its contents[2] he did not give him the text, and concealed altogether the additional protocol.[3] On receiving the news of the treaty Thiers was angry, but he was no more angry than his countrymen. France found herself isolated once more as in 1815, with Europe arrayed against her.[4] The Chambers became excited; the most conservative journals called upon the nation to maintain its honor; men talked of taking up again the struggle against Europe and of regaining the natural frontiers of the country—the Rhine and the Alps. Immense war preparations were begun, a credit of a hundred million francs being voted solely to put Paris in a state of proper defense.[5] Nevertheless, Louis Philippe was resolved not to go to war, and he used every means to obtain some concession from the allies by which he could honorably re-enter the European concert. He worked particularly through his son-in-law, Leopold of Belgium, who was also an uncle of Queen Victoria and had great influence with her.[6] Palmerston, however, declared to Guizot that, while the French government might re-enter the European concert, the treaty would be literally carried out.[7] This reply was, at the moment, all the more provoking, because Thiers' agent in Egypt, Count

[1] Hertslet's *Map of Europe by Treaty*, vol. ii, p. 1008.

[2] Guizot, *Embassy to the Court of St. James*, chap. v, p. 208.

[3] See Palmerston's defense of his action in his letter to Hobhouse in Bulwer, *Life of Palmerston*, vol. iii, p. 426.

[4] Guizot, *Embassy to the Court of St. James*, chap. v, pp. 235 *et seq.*

[5] *Annual Register*, 1840, p. 171 *et seq.*

[6] Guizot, *Embassy to the Court of St. James*, chap. v, pp. 263 *et seq.*

[7] Guizot, *Embassy to the Court of St. James*, chap. v, pp. 272 *et seq.*

Walewski, had just returned with a concession from Mehemet, who had promised him to accept the hereditary possession of Egypt and the life possession of Syria.[1] Thiers immediately sent Walewski to Constantinople to obtain the assent of the Porte to this arrangement, and on September 18, 1840, announced that France would make no further concessions, and was ready to sustain her position.[2]

These declarations alarmed the more yielding members of the British Cabinet,[3] but Palmerston persisted in his calm assurance that Louis Philippe would not go to war and that Mehemet would not resist the allies. At this conjuncture news arrived from the East which tended to defeat any attempt at conciliation. Whilst a Turkish agent carried the ultimatum of the treaty to Mehemet, and before the latter's reply had arrived at Constantinople, an Anglo-Austrian fleet blockaded the coast of Syria and bombarded Beyrouth, which was evacuated by Ibrahim September 11th. Three days later, the Divan, instead of accepting the proposition of Walewski, outlawed Mehemet. When the news from the East arrived at Paris, there occurred another outburst of indignation, and talk of fighting Europe and regaining the Rhine frontier was again indulged in.[4] This was met by a patriotic outburst all over Germany, where demands were on all sides heard for a campaign against the hereditary enemy, such as had been made in 1813. Prussia and Austria consulted as to the best measures of defense, and the situation became very critical.[5]

Several circumstances, however, combined to prevent an outbreak, the principal one being the determination of Louis

[1] Guizot, *Embassy to the Court of St. James*, chap. v, p. 295 *et seq.*

[2] Bulwer, *Life of Palmerston*, vol. ii, p. 283.

[3] Hansard's *Parliamentary Debates*, vol. liii, p. 182 *et seq.*, and vol. lvi, p. 50 *et seq.*

[4] Guizot, *Embassy to the Court of St. James*, chap. v, p. 322 *et seq.*

[5] As to the war alarm in Germany, see *Aus Metternich's Nachgelassenen Papieren*, vol. vi, p. 465 *et seq.*

Philippe to avoid war. When, therefore, early in October, Thiers submitted a warlike declaration to the Chambers, Louis Philippe refused to support it. Thiers resigned, but he was prevailed upon to withdraw his resignation when shown that in the excited state of public feeling it might prove fatal to the monarchy. He recalled the French fleet from the East in order to prevent a collision with the British, and limited the *casus belli* to the contingency of the quadruple alliance depriving Mehemet of Egypt.[1] Metternich, who did not want war any more than Louis Philippe, worked on Palmerston, who, under the pressure of his colleagues as well as of Metternich, gave an assurance that the outlawry of Mehemet should have no effect.[2] Metternich at the same time interceded with Louis Philippe to get rid of Thiers, whom he regarded as the incarnation of the Revolution and whom Louis Philippe himself was anxious to dismiss as soon as he safely could do so. An attempt on Louis Philippe's life having momentarily revived his popularity, he seized the opportunity to dismiss Thiers, because of the latter's refusal to moderate the address to the Chambers and accept a colorless one proposed by the king himself.[3] Marshal Soult became president of the new ministry, but Guizot, who became minister of foreign affairs, was the real head.[4]

The new ministry set before itself the task of reconciling France with Europe without suffering a loss of dignity. Guizot hoped that the European courts would be willing to concede to him what they had refused to Thiers, because of his known conservative views. Leopold of Belgium was again employed as an intermediary to obtain some concessions from the terms of the treaty of the 15th of July, but

[1] *Annual Register*, 1840, p. 177; also Guizot, *Embassy to the Court of St. James*, chap. vi, p. 321.

[2] Guizot, *Embassy to the Court of St. James*, chap. vi, p. 321.

[3] Guizot, *Embassy to the Court of St. James*, chap. vii, p. 381.

[4] *Annual Register*, 1840, p. 178.

Palmerston answered that the interests of Europe could not be sacrificed to those of Louis Philippe, and that France in any event had nothing to do with a treaty to which she was not a party.[1] At about the same time word arrived from the East that nearly all the coast of Syria had surrendered to the English fleet, St. Jean d' Acre having done so on November 2d, and that Ibrahim had been compelled to evacuate most of Syria. In such a crisis it was felt that no French ministry, however desirous of peace, could yield without sacrificing French dignity. In the parliamentary discussions of November 25th to 28th Guizot declared that France would not suffer Mehemet to be dispossessed of Egypt, and the armaments begun by the preceding ministry were continued with feverish haste.

And the reports which continued to come from the East were such as to prevent the French government from assuming any other position. After the taking of St. Jean d'Acre, Admiral Napier had sailed to Alexandria and threatened it with bombardment if Mehemet did not make an immediate submission. Mehemet, deserted by France, agreed to the convention of November 25th, which stipulated that, in consideration of the complete evacuation of Syria by Ibrahim, and the restitution of the Turkish fleet, the quadruple alliance would cease all warlike operations against Mehemet and induce the Ottoman Porte to concede to him the hereditary possession of Egypt. The effect of this action, which was consistent with the view now held by the French government, was entirely nullified by the course of the Porte, which, under the influence of Ponsonby, the English ambassador at Constantinople, rejected the convention and refused to grant to Mehemet more than the life possession of Egypt.[2] The Eastern question became more acute than ever. However desirous the French government might be to avoid a conflict,

[1] Letter to Granville in Bulwer, *Life of Palmerston*, vol. ii, p. 301.

Annual Register, 1840, p. 193.

it could not disarm without dishonor.   The troops were kept on a war footing, and on February 1, 1841, the Chambers passed a law relative to the fortification of Paris.

The resolute attitude of France alarmed Austria and Prussia. Metternich was more anxious than ever to prevent war and maintain the status quo in Europe, and Prussia was fearful for her Rhine provinces.[1]   The danger would not be removed until France disarmed, and that would be impossible until the Eastern question was solved.   Austria and Prussia therefore labored together during January, 1841, to bring France once more into the European concert; and in spite of the under-handed opposition of Nicholas and the indifference of Palmerston, the quadruple alliance was persuaded to come to an agreement acceptable to France.   The allies adopted on January 31, 1841, a note inviting the Porte not only to revoke the outlawry pronounced against Mehemet, but also to accord to him the promise that his descendants in the direct line should be successively named by the Sultan to the pashalik of Egypt. This was far removed from the demands of France a year before, but it was at least a concession, and Guizot eagerly embraced it.   He therefore authorized Bourqueney, the French ambassador at London, to accept the terms embodied in the note of the 31st of January, but only on the following conditions : That the initiative in the negotiations should be taken not by France but by the allies ; that the hereditary possession of Egypt should be assured to Mehemet Ali ; that the treaty of the 15th of July should be considered as entirely executed, and should not again be brought into discussion ; that its fulfilment should be evidenced by an official notice to the French government ; and that the question of disarmament should not be raised.   These points admitted, the French government would gladly conclude a convention relative to the East with the allies.[2]

[1] *Aus Metternich's Nachgelassenen Papieren*, vol. vi, pp. 513 *et seq.*

[2] Debidour, *Histoire Diplomatique*, vol. i, p.

The preliminary conditions demanded by Guizot were accepted, and in the first week of March a protocol was drawn up. The treaty of the 15th of July was declared to be fulfilled, and a project of a quintuple convention was submitted. This project was far from what Guizot desired. It consisted simply in a declaration that the Straits should rest under the absolute sovereignty of Turkey and should be closed to the naval forces of all the other powers. Guizot wished to include in it a guarantee of the integrity and independence of the Ottoman Empire, but to this Russia now refused to accede. He also desired to insert a provision for the protection of the Christians in Syria, but this point England was unwilling to discuss. Nevertheless, Guizot was about to accept the protocol when grave news arrived from the East. The Sultan by a Hatti-sheriff of February 13th had accorded to Mehemet the hereditary possession of Egypt, but at the instigation of Ponsonby had imposed restrictions which Mehemet would not accept. The Sultan was to have the right on each vacancy to designate among the heirs of Mehemet the new titulary of the pashalik; the Pasha was to reduce his army to eighteen thousand men, and was not to name any officer above the rank of adjutant; the mode of collecting the taxes was to be prescribed by the Sultan, who was to receive one-fourth of the proceeds.[1] Mehemet refused these conditions, and Guizot declared that France could not sign the projected convention. None of the powers, however, was desirous to uphold the Porte in its position. Metternich interposed with energy at Constantinople, and on April 19th another Hatti-sheriff was issued satisfactory to Mehemet.[2] The hereditary possession of Egypt was to be according to primogeniture; the Pasha was to be permitted to name the officers of the army up to the grade of colonel, inclusive; and finally he was to pay a tribute, the amount of which was to be fixed from time to time. On June 10th,

[1] *Annual Register*, 1841, p. 286.
[2] *Annuaire Lesur*, 1841, p. 516.

Mehemet solemnly accepted the conditions of the Hatti-sheriff, and on July 13, 1841, there was concluded at London a treaty which guaranteed the neutrality of the Straits.[1] It did not by any means solve the Eastern question. In his effort to abase France, Nicholas had lost the ground which he gained by the Treaty of Unkiar Skelessi, and he set to work to recover it; but he was to find in the future that no one state would be allowed to settle the Eastern question alone.

Sultan Abdul-Medjid, who succeeded Mahmoud in 1839, placed himself to a great extent under the influence of Reschid Pasha, the leader of the Turkish reform party. Reschid, in turn, was largely controlled by Stratford Canning, who from this time down to the Crimean War was to exercise so great an influence on the fortunes of the Ottoman Empire.[2] Reschid and his friends believed that the only way to prevent the destruction of their country was by carrying out the reforms inaugurated by Mahmoud and developing them. In 1839 there was published the Hatti-sheriff of Gulhané,[3] which proposed many reforms in administration, education and taxation, and in the relations between the Turks and the Rayahs. Reschid exerted himself, as far as possible, in the face of Turkish fanaticism and Rayah ignorance, to put it into force; but he was obliged to combat an enemy who was quite as difficult to deal with as either of the other two. This enemy was Nicholas of Russia. The Czar did not desire to see the Ottoman Empire regenerated, and he used all his influence with the subject peoples to prevent it. In 1844, he paid a visit to England, ostensibly to congratulate Victoria on her accession to the throne, but incidentally to destroy the *entente* between England and France, and to come to some agreement with Great Britain on the Turkish question. It was during this visit that

[1] Hertslet, *Map of Europe by Treaty*, vol. ii, p. 1024.

[2] Lane Poole, *Life of Stratford Canning*, chaps. xvii. to xxiii.

[3] *British and Foreign State Papers*, vol. xxxi, p. 1239.

he made his first suggestion for the dismemberment of the Ottoman Empire. It was received very coldly by the British foreign office.[1] Whatever the immediate plans which he may have had against the integrity of Turkey, he was obliged to postpone them. Soon afterwards there came the Revolution of 1848; and the attitude of the Porte during that struggle was not such as to conciliate him. The Porte witnessed with satisfaction the rebellions in its neighbors' dominions, and seized the opportunity of an uprising in the Danubian principalities to send an army thither, ostensibly to keep the peace, but in reality to counterbalance the Russian army which had also occupied the territory. And when, after the revolution was over, Russia and Austria demanded the extradition of the Polish and Hungarian refugees, who had found asylum in the Turkish dominions, the Porte, strongly backed by France and England, refused either their extradition or their immediate expulsion.[2] It was galling to Nicholas to submit to such a denial by his weak neighbor, but he was only biding his time. By 1852, the European situation appearing to be favorable, he determined to carry out the scheme which he had never relinquished since his accession to the throne—the despoilment of the Ottoman Empire.

[1] Nesselrode's memorandum, containing the views of Nicholas and delivered to the British government, is printed in *Parliamentary Papers* for 1854, vol. lxxi, part vi.

[2] See the voluminous correspondence on this question in *British and Foreign State Papers*, vol. xxxviii, p. 1266 *et seq.*

CHAPTER VI

THE CRIMEAN WAR

THE special privileges enjoyed by the Latin monks in the Holy Places in the East, under the protection of France, dated back to the sixteenth century. These privileges were solemnly confirmed by the Capitulations of 1740. But since 1701, when Peter the Great became not only the temporal but also the spiritual head of Russia, the encroachments of the Greek monks on the privileges of the Latins had been steady and persistent. After the death of Louis XV., the attention of French statesmen was turned chiefly to internal affairs, and from the French Revolution to the accession of Napoleon III., the governmental changes were so violent and numerous that the Latin monks could rely but little on the support of the chief Catholic power, while the Greeks were always sure of the aid of Russia. When Louis Napoleon became President of France, the chief of the Holy Places, the Holy Sepulchre, as well as the great church of Bethlehem, the grotto of the Nativity, and the tomb of the Virgin at Gethsemane, had fallen into the hands of the Greeks. Louis Napoleon desired to gain the support of the Church. To this end he overthrew the Roman Republic, and he now decided to intervene in the dispute as to the Holy Places. After having vainly invoked the Capitulations of 1740, he demanded the appointment of a commission to inquire into the relative claims of the Greeks and Latins. The Sultan appointed such a commission, July 15, 1851. After several months of investigation, the commission reported in favor of the claims of France, and this report was confirmed by the firman of February 9, 1852. But, profiting by the absence of the French ambassador, Russia intimidated the Porte into granting demands irreconcilable with the firman. At the same time, official Russia began to claim that the Treaty of Kainardji not only made the Czar the legal protector of the Greek monks, but also of all subjects of the Ottoman Porte belonging to the Greek Church.[1]

In his efforts to give effect to this claim, Nicholas counted on the benevolent neutrality of Austria, because of her gratitude for his suppression of the Hungarian Revolution, and also on that of Prussia, because of the firm friendship of Frederick William IV. Hating France as the source of all revolutionary movements, he despised Napoleon III., and if it were necessary to fight France in order to carry out his projects, he would not hesitate to do so, provided he could placate England.[2] His efforts were, therefore, directed to that end, and in January, 1853, he held the celebrated conversations with Sir Hamilton Seymour. Likening Turkey to a "sick man"—a man in a dying condition—he suggested that it behooved Russia and England to consider his demise and arrange for the distribution of his effects. The thing could be done quietly and easily, provided Russia and England could agree. He was willing that England should have Egypt and Crete, and, although he disclaimed any desire to retain Constantinople permanently, he would occupy it temporarily as a gage for the future.[3] The Czar's proposals were rejected by the English ministry; but it seems quite certain that, almost until war actually broke out, Nicholas labored under the impression that England was not

[1] See *Parliamentary Papers for 1854*, vol. lxxi, nos. 1–84. See also in Phillimore's *International Law*, third edition, vol. i, page 618 *et seq.*, a thorough discussion of the Russian claim to a protectorate over the Christians in the Ottoman Empire.

[2] For an account of Nicholas' feelings toward France, see Rambaud, *Histoire de la Russie*, vol. ii, chap. xvi.

[3] "Nous avons sur les bras un homme malade—un homme gravement malade; ce sera, je vous le dis franchement, un grand malheur si, un de ces jours, il devait nous échapper, surtout avant que toutes les dispositions nécessaires fussent prises."

opposed to the destruction of the Ottoman Empire, and that she had declined his overtures probably because she had some scheme of partition of her own.

On February 10, 1853, Prince Mentschikoff, one of the highest dignitaries of Russia, set out for Constantinople on a special embassy. On the way south he visited the Russian fleet and inspected the army along the Pruth, and with the commander of the forces and the vice-admiral of the fleet he entered Constantinople February 28th. In response to inquiries as to the object of the special embassy, Nesselrode assured foreign representatives that it was to discuss the two questions that had recently arisen in consequence of the dispute as to the Holy Places in Palestine and of the rebellion in Montenegro.[1] No one could have been selected more fit to carry out an arrogant mission than Prince Mentschikoff, than whom there was no more arrogant man. Neither France nor England had at the moment an ambassador in Constantinople; but towards the end of March the Turkish ministers informed the chargés d'affaires of the western powers that Mentschikoff had made a proposal under threat of evil consequences if it were divulged. In exchange for a permanent alliance which he offered the Sultan, he demanded that the Sultan should conclude a treaty recognizing the Czar as the legal protector of the Greek church in the Ottoman Empire.[2] As the heads of that church exercised numerous and important temporal functions over the 12,000,000 Christian subjects of the Ottoman Porte, the submission of the Sultan to this demand would have been practically equivalent to an abdication of all sovereignty.

The English and French ambassadors, Sir Stratford Canning and M. de la Cour, soon reached Constantinople. Their governments had been advised of the situation and had instructed them to act in unison. Canning and de la Cour affected to

[1] Seymour to Russell, *Parliamentary Papers*, vol. lxxi, nos. 87, 124, 171.

[2] For details of negotiations, see *Parliamentary Papers*, vol. lxxi, nos. 108–140.

believe what Mentschikoff continued to assert, that the object of the latter's mission was the settlement of questions as to the Holy Places and Montenegro; and they hoped by peaceably settling these questions to deprive Russia of any pretext for further interference in Turkey.   Thanks to Austrian pressure at Constantinople, the Montenegrin question was already in a fair way to be settled,[1] and Canning had no great difficulty in obtaining from France such concessions in the Holy Places dispute as necessarily satisfied Russia.[2]   An agreement was signed May 4th, and there was now nothing left to Mentschikoff but either to withdraw or to unmask.   Nicholas did not hesitate.   By his order Mentschikoff on the 5th of May addressed an ultimatum to the Porte drawn up in most concise terms, demanding that the Porte conclude within five days a convention with Russia guaranteeing to the Greek church not only its religious liberties, but also its temporal privileges. If the answer were in the negative, he should immediately quit Constantinople and his master would take the necessary measures.[3]

Encouraged by the French and English ambassadors the Porte replied, on May 10th, that it could not agree to a convention which would destroy its independence by placing its internal administration under the surveillance and control of a foreign power.   It was willing to guarantee by a public act full religious liberty to all its subjects.   But that would be as an act of sovereignty; it would not engage itself in that respect with any foreign power.   Still less would it bind itself by contract in anything that concerned the temporal privileges of the Greek church.[4]   The Sultan at the same time confirmed his refusal by putting Rechid Pasha, the reformer and enemy of Russia, in charge of foreign affairs.   Mentschikoff professed

[1] Hansard's *Parliamentary Debates*, vol. cxxvi, p. 371 *et seq.*

[2] Lane-Poole, *Life of Stratford Canning*, vol. ii, chap. xxv.

[3] *Parliamentary Papers*, vol. lxxi, no. 179.

[4] *Ibid.*, vol. lxxi, no. 193.

to reduce his pretensions by suggesting that instead of a formal convention, a simple note should be addressed to the Russian government, in which the Porte should make the concessions demanded.[1] Rechid, on the same day, May 20, 1853, sent a note drawn in a sense directly the opposite of that which Mentschikoff suggested, carefully reserving the independence and sovereignty of the Sultan. Mentschikoff left Constantinople the next day. A few days later Nesselrode sent an ultimatum to the Porte demanding that it accept Mentschikoff's last proposal within eight days, after which, if it persisted in its refusal, the Czar "would take his guarantee" and immediately occupy Moldavia and Wallachia. On June 11th, Nesselrode addressed a circular to all Russian diplomatic agents abroad, in which he explained the "irresistible" reasons which had driven Nicholas to that extreme.[2]

Europe was greatly stirred, and was almost a unit against the Czar; but the provocation to England and France was especially great, for Nicholas had given his word to the English Government that he would not act in the East without first coming to an agreement with it.[3] The two western powers daily drew closer together, and on June 1st they ordered their fleets to Besika Bay, just outside the Dardanelles. By so doing they still observed the Treaty of the Straits of 1841, and yet were within call of the Sultan. This enraged the Czar, who was already incensed at the rejection of Nesselrode's ultimatum, and at the issuance by the Porte on June 6th of a hatti-sheriff, which secured full religious liberty to all the subjects of the Sultan.[4] On June 26th, Nicholas issued a manifesto to the Russian nation, justifying his action as the performance of a sacred duty.[5] On July 3d,

---

[1] *Parliamentary Papers*, vol. lxxi, no. 210.

[2] *Ibid.*, vol. lxxi, no. 236.

[3] For repeated assurances, see *Parliamentary Papers*, vol. lxxi, no. 195.

[4] *Parliamentary Papers*, vol. lxxi, no. 323.

[5] *Ibid.*, vol. lxxi, no. 316.

the Russian troops occupied the principalities, though Nesselrode assured the foreign representatives that the Czar did not
consider himself in a state of war with Turkey, but sought
merely to take his guarantees.[1]

The statesmen and diplomatists of Europe who had striven
so hard since the Revolution of 1848 to prevent a breach of
the peace, now set to work to modify the situation by the usual
methods of diplomacy.   Austria, who had more at stake than
other powers, and whose sympathies moreover were divided
by her interests, labored with particular energy.   Besides
being deeply indebted to Nicholas for his assistance against
the Hungarians, she approved of his system of government.
On the other hand, she feared a Napoleon in France; and she
was alienated both from England and from France by their
sympathy with Hungary and their support of Turkey in her
refusal to deliver up the Hungarian refugees.   But Russian
control of the Danube would greatly endanger her interests,
and the Czar could easily arouse a Pan-Slavic agitation at any
time in the Hapsburg dominions.   In order not to irritate the
Czar, who despite the treaty of 1841 did not recognize any
right of Europe to interfere between him and Turkey, Count
Buol, the Austrian chancellor, offered to him simply a semi-
official mediation, which the Czar, always hopeful of retaining
Austrian friendship, accepted.   Buol also persuaded the Porte
to reply to the Russian occupation of the principalities by a
simple protest, instead of by a declaration of war.[2]   Then, in
order to bring England and France into the negotiations, he
called together the ambassadors at Vienna, of England,
France and Prussia, into an unofficial conference.   Nearly
every European statesman had a solution of the difficulty, and
at least eleven different plans were seriously considered, but
on August 1st the conference finally agreed to what is known
as the Vienna note, which was forthwith transmitted to the

---

[1] *Parliamentary Papers*, vol. lxxi, no. 325.

[2] *Ibid.*, vol. lxxi, no. 368.

Czar and to the Sultan. The note was vague and equivocal, and the Czar immediately accepted it.[1] But when it reached Constantinople it was closely scrutinized by both Rechid and Stratford Canning, who thought that they discerned in it a fatal defect, in that it omitted all mention of the essential point of the controversy, the maintenance of the sovereignty of the Ottoman Porte. The Turkish government therefore refused to accept the note, unless it were amended.[2]

For a moment, the sympathy of Europe was withdrawn from the Turk, but on September 7th Nicholas published an interpretation of the Vienna note which fully justified the Turkish action.[3] The conferring diplomatists at Vienna were compelled to admit that the Czar's interpretation was not what had been intended, and France and England a few weeks later ordered their fleets to pass the Dardanelles. During all these months Turkey had been preparing for war. Mussulman fanaticism had been aroused by the crusading tone of Nicholas' manifesto, and the Porte could no longer withstand the popular outcry. When the Anglo-French fleet appeared before Constantinople a great Council was held, and ten days later, on October 4th, war was solemnly declared by the Porte against Russia.[4] October 8th, Omar Pasha summoned Prince Gortchakoff to evacuate the principalities, on pain of beginning hostilities, in fifteen days.

Nicholas was not moved by the warlike attitude of Turkey. He believed that the financial bankruptcy of the country would render it incapable of maintaining a war for six months. Moreover, he still counted on the neutrality of Austria and Prussia, and the fancied impossibility of an alliance between England and France. Accordingly he was in no hurry to begin operations, and Nesselrode informed Europe October

[1] *Parliamentary Papers*, vol. lxxi, part 2, no. 54.

[2] *Ibid.*, vol. lxxi, part 2, nos. 66–79 *passim*, especially enclosure in no. 71.

[3] *Ibid.*, vol. lxxi, part 2, no. 94.

[4] See the declaration in Hertslet, *Map of Europe by Treaty*, vol. ii, p. 1171.

30th that Russia, although she accepted the war which had been forced upon her, would prove the purity of her intentions by confining herself to the defensive.[1]   His pacific language encouraged the Vienna conferrees, who resumed their consultations, and on December 5th adopted a protocol as a point of departure for securing peace.   It specified two conditions as being essential to the European equilibrium: (1) The integrity of the Ottoman empire, and (2) the governmental independence of the Sultan; but the Sultan was to be asked to ameliorate the condition of his Christian subjects.   A note was added to the protocol by which the Porte was requested to make known the conditions on which it would treat with Russia.[2]

Just at this moment, when everything looked propitious, events occurred which destroyed all hope of peace.   Contrary to the Czar's expectations, the Turks were generally successful in their military operations and defeated the Russians in both Europe and Asia.   This so angered Nicholas that he abandoned his pacific declaration of October 30th and ordered his fleet to sea.   It found the Turkish fleet in the harbor of Sinope, on the coast of Asia Minor, and utterly destroyed it.[3] The Sultan, being thus disabled from defending himself in the Black Sea, begged the French and English admirals to pass the Bosphorus.[4]   The French government was ready to grant this petition, since it had already determined upon war;[5] but the peace cabinet of Aberdeen tried, though in vain, to stem the tide of English public feeling.[6]   Palmerston's resignation

[1] *Parliamentary Papers*, vol. lxxi, part 2, no. 226, inclosure 1.

[2] *Ibid.*, vol. lxxi, part 2, no. 315, inclosure 2.

[3] *Ibid.*, vol. lxxi, part 2, no. 317.

[4] *Ibid.*, vol. lxxi, part 2, no. 337.

[5] Napoleon III. wished to divert the attention of the French from home affairs, and hoped by a successful foreign war to strengthen his hold on the throne.

[6] "The public here is furiously Turkish and anti-Russian," the Prince Consort wrote to Baron Stockmar September 21st, 1853.   Martin, *Life of the Prince Consort*, vol. ii, p. 416.

from the cabinet was accepted, but a few days later Aberdeen
was forced to re-admit him and to adopt his program.[1] On
December 27th the two western courts informed Russia that
their fleets would enter the Black Sea and that the Russian
fleet would not be permitted to sail there.[2] On the 30th of
the same month Turkey informed Buol that the conditions
upon which she was willing to re-establish peace were (1) the
maintenance and guarantee of the territorial integrity of the
Ottoman Empire; (2) the evacuation of the principalities by
Russia; (3) the renewal of the guarantees given to the Porte
in 1841, and (4) respect for the governmental independence of
the Sultan, who should not refuse new concessions to his
Christian subjects, but should grant them as an act of
sovereignty. On these conditions Turkey was willing to open
negotiations under the mediation of the Vienna conference.[3]
The conference immediately acted upon the Turkish program,
and on January 13, 1854, charged Buol to submit it to the
Czar. Everybody anxiously awaited his decision, but the
Czar was now desirous of gaining time. Relieved of all illu-
sions as to the position of England,[4] he was all the more
anxious to be assured as to the attitude of Austria and Prussia. He sent Count Orloff to Vienna and Baron Budberg to
Berlin to secure the benevolent neutrality of those two courts,
promising in return that he would consult with them and with
them only as to the re-establishment of the political equilibrium
in the East.[5] Both envoys were unsuccessful, and the Czar
refused the Turkish proposals. Napoleon III. on January
29th wrote an autograph letter to Nicholas, inviting him to
evacuate the principalities and to submit the future treaty of

[1] Ashley, *Life of Palmerston*, vol. ii, chap. ii.

[2] *Parliamentary Papers*, vol. lxxi, part 2, no. 345.

[3] *Ibid.*, vol. lxxi, part 2, no. 396.

[4] Nicholas had really thought that England had joined the Peace Society.
Chap. xxvi, McCarthy, *History of Our Own Times*.

[5] *Parliamentary Papers*, vol. lxxi, part 7, no. 31.

peace to the guarantee of Europe. Nicholas, who declined to call Napoleon III. "mon frère," answered his "bon ami" with a refusal, coupled with the assurance that Russia would be able to take care of herself in 1854, as she had been in 1812.[1] This pointed reference to the Moscow campaign did much to rouse the French, with whom the prospect of war was as yet unpopular.

England and France now addressed themselves with redoubled energy to the task of converting the coalition into a quadruple alliance, if possible. It was deemed especially important to gain Austria, for without her co-operation they could attack Russia only by way of the Baltic and the Black Sea, and that would mean a long and costly war before Russia could be exhausted. But Buol was unwilling to sign anything till France and England had gone too far to withdraw. So he suggested that they address an ultimatum to the Czar requiring the immediate evacuation of the principalities and threatening war in case of refusal.[2] He also considered it necessary for Austria, in case she should take part in the war, to secure the safety of her dominions by an alliance with Prussia; and with this aim he approached the Prussian court. He was in reality playing a double game. He hoped to push France and England to the front to do the fighting, and then to appear as an armed mediator between the belligerents and lay down the law for Europe. To the success of this design, also, the concurrence of Prussia was essential. Frederick William IV., however, was subject to contradictory influences. The Liberals of Prussia united with the Liberals of all Europe in detesting Nicholas for his part in the Hungarian Revolution; and many of the king's warmest friends, and the heir-

---

[1] The letter of Napoleon III. to Nicholas and the latter's answer are found in the *Annual Register for 1854*, p. 242 *et seq.*

[2] Clarendon to Westmoreland at Vienna, no. 103, and answer of Westmoreland, No. 106 of part 7, *Parliamentary Papers*. Also the British demand for the evacuation of the principalities, no. 101.

apparent, Prince William, were strong for an English alliance. On the other hand, the reactionaries led by the Queen were favorable to Russia; while a third party, led by Bismarck, demanded a strict neutrality, contending that German interests were not involved, and that it should be the duty of Prussia to stand as the protector of German interests, while Austria looked after her selfish concerns.[1]   The King himself sympathized more with the Czar than with the allies.   A strongly religious man, he looked upon the Czar as the defender of the Cross against the Crescent, and he hated and feared Napoleon III.   But at the same time Nicholas was the disturber of the peace, and Frederick William did not desire to offend the other Protestant power, England.   His actions, therefore, during the period of negotiations, were vacillating, the result of the opposing influences to which he was subject.   In March, he declared he would never go to war with the Czar.   Then he hastened to send agents to London and Paris to explain his position and to give assurances that he was willing to sign a protocol with France, Austria and England which should afford a basis for re-establishing peace between Russia and Turkey.[2]

France and England meanwhile had completed their preparations, and could no longer delay to enter upon their campaign. March 12th they concluded an offensive and defensive alliance with Turkey.[3]   March 27th they declared war against Russia;[4] and on April 10th they formally united in a treaty by which they engaged that neither of them would treat separately with

---

[1] The positions of the various Prussian parties on the question of alliance with the Western Powers are well stated in Von Sybel, *Founding of the German Empire*, book vi, chap. ii.

[2] As to the irritation felt in the West at the vacillating policy of Prussia during the war, a policy of great advantage to Russia, see *Debates in Parliament for 1854-1856*, especially that of March 20, 1855, in Hansard's *Parliamentary Debates*, vol. cxxxvii, p. 858 *et seq.*

[3] Hertslet, vol. ii, p. 1181.

[4] *Ibid.*, vol. ii, p. 1185.

Russia or seek in the war any individual advantage.[1] On April 9th, the conference of Vienna accepted the suggestion of the King of Prussia and adopted a protocol which seemed to establish a strict solidarity between the four states in all that concerned the East.[2] Each engaged not to separate itself from the other three for the settlement of the pending difficulties, and they adopted as an invariable basis for such a settlement the four following conditions: (1) The integrity of the Ottoman Empire; (2) the evacuation of the principalities by Russia; (3) the independence of the Sultan and the free gift by him of liberties and privileges to his Christian subjects, and (4) an agreement on the guarantees necessary to regulate the political relations of Turkey in such a manner as to safeguard the European equilibrium. Nicholas in the meantime had not been idle. He had endeavored to obtain the alliance of either Sweden or Denmark, but having failed in the attempt, was exposed to an attack from the Baltic. He had also been unsuccessful in inciting Persia to a war with the Sultan. He was more fortunate with Greece, who directly aided the Christian insurrection in Thessaly and Epirus. But this eventually proved to be of little value, for France and England sent ships and troops to the Piraeus and easily restrained Greece.

Frederick William meanwhile became alarmed at Prussia's isolation in Europe and lent a willing ear to the Austrian proposal for an alliance, and on April 20, 1854, a treaty was signed,[3] by which Austria and Prussia agreed both to repel any hostile attack on the territory of either. Bismarck, however, deprived the treaty of its effect by obtaining a stipulation for its submission to the German Confederation. Bismarck sought to gain the gratitude of Russia without compromising Prussia with the western powers. He knew how slowly the German Diet acted, and he also knew that many of the princes of the smaller Ger-

---

[1] Hertslet, vol. ii, p. 1193.

[2] *Ibid.*, vol. ii, p. 1191.

[3] *Ibid.*, vol. ii, p. 1201.

man states were bound by matrimony and other ties to Russia.
The treaty, instead of benefiting Austria, would really injure
her. For if Austria should answer the English and French
demands for action with the statement that she could not act
without Prussia, Prussia could answer that she could not act
without the approval of the Confederation, and this it was an
easy matter to prevent. Austria would, thus have repaid the
Czar with ingratitude for past services, and, having also failed
to aid France and England, would become an object of dislike
to everybody. This was shrewd diplomacy, nor did it fail in
its object.[1] An additional article to the treaty stipulated: (1)
That Austria should summon the Czar to arrest his march
and to fix the terms of his occupation of the principalities, and
(2) that the two contracting parties should take the offensive
only in case the Russians crossed the Balkans or proclaimed
the annexation of the principalities. There was little danger
of Prussia's having to undertake war under those conditions,
for the Anglo-French forces had already arrived in Turkey,
and Nicholas, instead of taking the offensive, was preparing to
defend himself.

The slight value of the Austro-Prussian treaty was soon to
be demonstrated. After six weeks' delay, due largely to
Prussian procrastination, Buol sent the summons to Russia
June 3d. June 29th Nicholas sent his reply. He had decided
to prevent Austria from joining his enemies, but he answered
that he could not formally comply with the summons unless
Austria would guarantee him against attack by way of the
principalities. As a matter of fact his troops had almost completed the evacuation of them; and on June 14th Austria had
contracted an alliance with Turkey[2] to the effect that to the
end of the war Austria should occupy and defend if necessary,
against all attack, Moldavia and Wallachia, but in so doing
should not hinder the operations of the allies against Russia.

[1]Debidour, *Histoire Diplomatique de l'Europe*, vol. ii. chap. iv.

[2] Hertslet, vol ii, p. 1213.

Austria sent her troops into the principalities and called upon Prussia and the Confederation to prepare their contin· gents, but both Prussia and the Confederation, which had finally acceded to the Austro-Prussian Treaty on July 24th, answered that the Russian reply to the summons was per- fectly satisfactory, and that, if Russia should be compelled to evacuate the principalities, the allies also should be obliged to stay out of them. Moreover, Prussia declared that as the Czar had not crossed the Balkans· or announced the annexa- tion of the principalities, she was exempt from the engagement to undertake war against him. Buol was finally left stranded. He could neither demand of the allies what Prussia and the Confederation desired, nor could he join the allies without Prussia's support. But as the Russians had evacuated the principalities, and as it was too late in the summer to begin without Austria's coöperation a campaign in Russia, France and England decided not to cross the Danube. The expedi- tion to the Crimea was, however, agreed upon, and it was hoped that Sebastopol could be taken by a coup de main.

Despite the determination of the allies to continue the war and abase Russia, the diplomats did not relinquish their efforts to bring about a peace ; and when Buol reopened the Vienna conference in July, France and England took part in it, though Prussia declined to do so. August 8, 1854, the repre- sentatives of the three powers—Austria, England, and France —adopted the propositions which soon became known as the Four Points, along the lines of which the Treaty of Peace was eventually effected.[1] These were (1) that the protectorate exercised by Russia up to that time over Moldavia, Wallachia and Servia should cease, and that the privileges accorded by the Sultans to these provinces, as dependencies of the Otto- man Empire, should be put under the collective guarantee of the powers by a treaty concluded with the Porte ; (2) that the navigation of the Danube at its mouths should be freed from

[1] Hertslet, vol. ii, page 1216.

all obstacles, and made subject to the application of the principles of the Congress of Vienna; (3) that the Treaty of the
Straits of 1841 should be revised by the high contracting
powers in the interests of the balance of power of Europe;
and (4) that Russia should abandon her claim to exercise an
official protectorate over the subjects of the Sublime Porte, no
matter to what religion they belonged, and that the five great
powers should obtain from the Porte the confirmation and ob-
servance of the religious privileges of the different Christian
communities, without prejudicing the dignity and independence of the Ottoman crown.   The three courts declared that
they would not take into consideration any proposition of
Russia which did not imply a full and entire adhesion to these
conditions, although Austria reserved a certain liberty of judg-
ment in case she should be forced to take part in the war.

The four points were received with disfavor at Berlin and at
Frankfort, whither they were sent by Buol, who asked that,
as Austria had occupied the principalities and might be attacked there by Russia, Prussia and the confederation should,
conformably to the treaty of April 20th, mobilize their troops
for her protection.   The Prussian and German statesmen
answered that that treaty extended only to a defense of Austria
in her own territory; that if she occupied the principalities
she did do so at her own risk; and that German interests were
in no way involved in the last two of the four points.[1]   France
and England now assumed an insistent attitude towards
Austria, and for a third time asked her to join them and put
an end to the war.   By a convention signed November 26,
1854, which was approved at Frankfort December 9th,
Prussia and the Confederation agreed to support Austria in
the principalities; but it was expressly stated that the convention was not an application of the treaty of April 20th, and
that the contracting parties engaged to support only the first
and second of the four points.   This convention, however, did

[1] See Von Sybel, *Founding of the German Empire*, book 6, chap. iii.

not relieve Austria of her predicament; and as she had hitherto refused to enter into the war without the support of Prussia, and Prussia declined to aid her without the concurrence of the Confederation, it is likely that the third request of the allies upon Austria would have been futile, had not a new actor appeared upon the scene.

Since the Revolution of 1848, Sardinia was the only state in Italy that had avoided the adoption of a reactionary policy and repelled the advances of Austria. It had become the abode of all the Italian patriots who hoped for national unity. It had also prospered greatly under its liberal constitution, had multiplied its industries, and had developed its commerce. In 1852, Victor Emanuel called to his aid as prime minister one of the greatest statesmen of the century, Count Cavour. Cavour saw that the overshadowing influence of Austria upon Italy could never be removed except by foreign aid, and he determined to gain the friendship if not the assistance of the western powers, by lending them for service in the Crimea the small but brave and well-equipped army which he had gathered together. Sardinia had no pressing individual grievances against Russia and was little interested in the Eastern question, but if she participated in the war she would have a seat in the Congress which would probably be called to end it. Then, with the aid of France and England, she would bring up the Italian question. In this she would hardly be opposed by Russia, who was incensed at Austria's ingratitude, nor by Prussia, who desired to substitute her own supremacy for that of Austria in Germany. Cavour in November, 1854, opened negotiations with England and France, looking towards an alliance.[1] Buol now saw that he must take decisive action, or at least must appear to do so. On December 2, 1854, he concluded a treaty[2] with France and England, by which it was agreed that Austria should not depart from the Four Points

[1] Godkin, *Life of Victor Emanuel*, chap. viii.
[2] Hertslet, vol. ii, p. 1221.

nor negotiate separately with Russia, but should defend the principalities if necessary; and that, if peace was not made between the allies and Russia by January 1st, "the high contracting powers will deliberate without delay upon effectual means for obtaining the object of their alliance."

Buol had no intention of fighting. By signing the treaty he had sought to satisfy France and England and to intimidate Russia, and on the strength of the convention of November 26th with Prussia, he still hoped to appear as an armed mediator. Prussia, now concerned at her own isolation, prevailed upon Nicholas to allow Prince Gortchakoff, the Russian representative to Austria, to participate in the Vienna conference on the basis of the Four Points. Gortchakoff suggested the opening of a conference in which Russia and Turkey should be represented, as well as the other powers. France and England agreed to this, but insisted that, in order to preclude any misunderstanding as to the meaning of the Four Points, Austria should join in an explanation of them. Austria assented, and on December 28th the three powers made known to Gortchakoff their interpretation of the four conditions, and demanded that, as a preliminary to the opening of any negotiation, he should accede to them.[1] January 7th he refused to do so, at the same time presenting a memoir wherein the Russian view of the conditions was set forth. An entire month was thus lost, and during that time Austria had given no evidence of an intention to carry out the treaty of December 2d. The allies were indignant at the excuses which she offered from time to time, and the negotiations with Sardinia, which had been practically dropped during December, were reopened in January. On January 26, 1853, a treaty of alliance between Sardinia and the allied belligerents was concluded.[2] By this treaty Sardinia entered into the war not as an auxiliary, but as an equal, and agreed to send to the Crimea an army of 15,000 men, which was

[1] Hertslet, vol. ii, p. 1225.

[2] *Ibid.*, vol. ii, p. 1228.

to remain under the orders of its own general. The army was sent, and it did valiant service with the French and the English.

Austria now pretended to act zealously in the direction of carrying out the treaty of December 2nd, and once more called upon Prussia and the confederation to mobilize their troops. But she was answered with reproaches for having concluded the treaty of December 2nd without having consulted Germany. Moreover Bismarck, who represented Prussia in the Diet, maintained that, instead of Germany being menaced from the East, she was really endangered from the West, and at his instigation the Diet not only categorically refused on January 30th the request of Austria, but on February 8th adopted a resolution for placing the Federal contingents on a war footing within their respective military divisions. This was in reality an answer to Napoleon III.'s known desire to carry the war into Russia by crossing Germany, and it effectually forestalled any such movement.[1]

During the winter of 1854–1855, the sufferings of the allies were very great and the siege of Sebastopol advanced but little.[2] At the rate of progress made so far, the war would last for years. Fortunately for Europe, Nicholas died March 2nd, a disappointed and grief-stricken man, and was succeeded by Alexander II. Though the latter issued a manifesto on the day of his accession in which he declared that he would preserve the integrity of his Empire and follow the traditions of his ancestors, he was nevertheless anxious for peace; and on March 10th Nesselrode addressed a circular to the courts of Europe expressing the sincere desire of the Czar to end the war.[3] The western powers, and especially France, which was tired of the ruinous struggle in the Crimea, were as desirous of peace as Russia; and on March 15th the conference of Vienna was re-opened with the Four Points as a basis of negotiation.

[1] See Von Sybel, book 6, chap. iii.

[2] Kinglake, *Invasion of the Crimea*, vol. vii, chap. viii, sixth edition.

[3] *Annual Register*, 1855, p. 199.

Prussia, who had previously held aloof from the conference, now expressed a desire to enter it. Her request was granted, but only on condition that she accept the treaty of December 2d as a preliminary, and agree to share with the other powers the consequences of a failure of the conference to effect a peace.[1] As she was unwilling to do this, the conference opened without her. At first it looked as if there would be smooth sailing. The representatives of Austria, Russia, France, England and Turkey found no difficulty in agreeing on the first and second points, as to the future status of the principalities and the freedom of the Danube. But when they came to the third point—the revision of the Straits Treaty so as to insure the balance of power in Europe—they were unable to reach a decision; and so important was it thought to be that this point should be well settled, that France sent Drouyn de Lhuys, and England Lord John Russell, as special representatives to the conference.

The western representatives found that Austria would not consent to submit to the conference a proposal for the neutralization of the Black Sea because she was sure that Russia would not accept it. On the other hand, Drouyn de Lhuys, who always wished to ally France with Austria, suggested a scheme which he felt sure would be acceptable to the latter, and the refusal of which she would be willing to make a casus belli. He proposed—and Russell supported him—that the number of vessels which Russia could maintain in the Black Sea should be limited. Buol expressed approval of the principle of limitation, but declined to make its refusal by Russia a casus belli. Gortchakoff was aware of this, and when the plan was proposed in conference he promptly rejected it as dishonoring to Russia. He also declared that, although Russia was willing to respect the integrity of the Ottoman Empire, she was not willing to guarantee it. Buol gave the

---

[1] Speech of Lord Clarendon in Hansard's *Parliamentary Debates*, vol. cxxxvii, p. 876.

representatives of France and England to understand that he was willing to sign with them an ultimatum to Russia based on the principle of counter-weights, *i, e.*, that Russia should be allowed to maintain whatever fleet she pleased in the Black Sea, and that Austria, England and France should have the right to keep there an equal force.   Although this seemed to involve no humiliation to Russia, and to leave the question of Ottoman integrity unsettled, Drouyn de Lhuys and Russell, despairing of obtaining anything better, accepted it.   Both were promptly disavowed by their governments.[1]   Napoleon III. felt that his throne would be in danger by such an inglorious ending of the war, and Palmerston refused to consider any such compromise.[2]   Austria then declared that she was no longer bound by the treaty of December 2d.   Her troops were withdrawn from the Russian frontier and reduced to a peace footing, and she definitely assumed a position of neutrality.   The conference was declared closed early in June, and it was evident that only war and not diplomacy would settle the question.[3]

France and England were exceedingly irritated by the attitude of Austria, and were determined to push the war with the greatest energy.   The forces besieging Sebastopol were increased, and on September 8th a general assault was made by the allies.   It was successful.   The effect produced on Europe was profound.   The people of the West rejoiced that the autocrat of the East, the enemy of liberalism, had been humbled.   Nevertheless, they wished for peace.   All the belligerent governments except France appeared to be otherwise disposed.   Naturally, the Ottoman Porte saw that the continuance of the

---

[1] Lord John Russell's explanation, *Parliamentary Debates*, vol. cxxxix, p. 559 *et seq.*

[2] For Palmerston's keen insight into Buol's game, see his letter to Lord John Russell in Ashley, *Life of Palmerston*, vol. ii, p. 84.

[3] The various protocols of the conference from March to June are found in *British and Foreign State Papers*, vol. xlv, pp. 54-118-124.

war would be beneficial to its interests. Sardinia also hoped
by its prolongation to create new claims to the friendship of
England and France. England especially seemed little disposed to peace. Having begun the war unprepared, her
losses had been enormous. But she had gradually repaired
her defects of organization and was anxious now for another
campaign, which she believed would be decisive, and in which
she hoped to satisfy the national pride, for most of the glory
in the taking of Sebastopol had gone to the French.[1] Public
opinion in France was strong for peace. The war had been
undertaken by the French without any feeling of hate. There
was more real friendship among the people for Russia than
for England, and Napoleon III had come out of the struggle
in a much stronger position both at home and abroad than he
had previously occupied. He, therefore, sought by every
means to bring the war to a close. He lent a friendly ear to
the advances of the Russian agents at Paris, but at the same
time concluded with England a defensive alliance with Sweden,
who hoped to recover Finland if the war should be prolonged.[2]
Though the Czar talked of upholding the honor of his country,
he was in reality more anxious for peace than any other of the
combatants. The distress in Russia was really terrible, and
the government dreaded another campaign in the coming
spring, in which it was sure to be worsted.

But, of all the European powers, Austria, though not a
party to the war, was the one most anxious for peace. Her
apprehensions were not confined to Turkey, but extended
equally to Italy, in whose political fate Napoleon III was ex-
hibiting an active and increasing interest. Shortly after the
fall of Sebastopol, Buol proposed to Napoleon the sending of
an ultimatum to Russia, the non-acceptance of which should
be regarded by Austria as a casus belli. He asked in return

---

[1] For British feeling on the war, see *Annual Register*, 1856, p. 1, and for French
feeling on the war, see *Annuaire Lesur*, 1855, p. 7.

[2] Hertslet, vol. ii, p. 1241.

for this action only that France and England should conclude with Austria a treaty for the maintenance of the integrity and independence of the Ottoman Empire, hoping thereby to render any further union of Russia with France and England impossible.[1]   The ultimatum was so drawn as to secure Austria's own interests, but to leave the status of the Black Sea to be settled by a convention between Turkey and Russia.   On the other hand, it required that Russia should accept the first and second of the Four Points, and, in order that she might be removed as far as possible from the mouth of the Danube, should give up Bessarabia.   Palmerston was indignant; in the first place, because he was not consulted, and in the second place, because the conditions which England considered most important were omitted.   He declared he did not intend to allow Austria to dictate terms of peace which England was to agree to without discussion.[2]   Louis Napoleon accepted Austria's project of an ultimatum, but early in December he received Victor Emanuel and Cavour with demonstrations of friendship, assuring them that he intended to see if something could not be done for Italy.   In the midst of these complications, peace became all the more necessary to Austria, and towards the middle of December she presented to England and France a draft of an ultimatum to be sent to Russia.   Should Russia fail to accept it by January 17th, Austria was to break off diplomatic relations with her and unite with the Western powers.   The ultimatum consisted of the Four Points with slight modifications, the principal one of which was the cession of Bessarabia by Russia to Moldavia; and a fifth point was added, to the effect that other matters of European interest might be discussed at a congress.   Alexander II., who, besides resenting the demand for the cession of territory, feared the introduction of unwelcome proposals under the fifth point, at first rejected the ultimatum; but his ministers soon convinced

[1] The treaty was afterwards concluded, Hertslet, vol. ii, p. 1280.

[2] Letter to Persigny, Ashley, *Life of Palmerston*, vol. ii, p. 103.

him that it would be impossible to face practically all Europe
with his treasury bankrupt. When, therefore, Frederic William IV., of Prussia, who still dreaded the possibility of being
driven from his neutral position, wrote him an autograph letter
urging him to accept the proffered terms, Alexander yielded
his adhesion to the Austrian ultimatum without reserve.

The proposed Congress met at Paris, February 25, 1856.[1]
There appeared at it representatives of Austria, England,
France, Russia, Sardinia and Turkey. Austria had secretly
endeavored to prevent the admission of Sardinia, but her efforts
were unsuccessful. Sweden, who had taken no part in the war,
did not ask to be represented. But Prussia, although she had
refused to participate in the struggle, sought to be represented
in order that she might avoid the appearance of isolation. Her
wishes were secretly antagonized by Austria, and were openly
opposed by England, who, with a view to make the conditions
for Russia as hard as possible, desired to exclude her friends
from the Congress.[2] Napoleon III., whom the King of Prussia
had called " the common enemy of Europe," was the only sovereign who really wished for Prussia's presence at the Congress. He desired to be on good terms with both Prussia and
Russia, since his plans with reference to Italy were adverse to the
interests of Austria. And as the Treaty of the Straits of 1841,
of which Prussia was a signatory, was to be renewed, it was
felt that Prussia's presence was really necessary, and accordingly, on March 16th, her representatives took their seats.

The Treaty of Paris of March 30, 1856, was based on the
Four Points, with various modifications and additions.[3] The
great work of Stratford Canning in the resuscitation of the
Ottoman Empire had culminated February 18th in the publi-

[1] For the various protocols to the Congress, see *British and Foreign State
Papers*, vol. xlvi, pp. 63–138.

[2] Letter of Prince Albert to King Leopold in Martin, *Life of the Prince Consort*,
vol. iii, chap. lxx.

[3] Hertslet, vol. ii, p. 1250 *et seq.*

cation by the Sultan of a Hatti-Humayoun, which, as an act of "his Sovereign will,"[1] accorded to the subject Christians the free exercise of their worship and promised a series of reforms that would regenerate the Ottoman Empire.[2] In recognition of this act, Article VII. of the treaty admitted the Porte " to participate in the advantages of the public law and concert of Europe." The powers also guaranteed the independence and territorial integrity of the Ottoman Empire, and agreed to consider any act tending to violate this engagement as a question of general interest. Article VIII. provided that if a dispute should arise between Turkey and one or more of the powers, they should, before appealing to arms, present the matter to the other contracting parties for their mediation. Article IX., which was to become famous in the later history of Turkey, declared that the Sultan, wishing to give a further proof of his generous intentions, had resolved to communicate to the contracting parties his Hatti-Humayoun of February, but that it was "clearly understood" that this communication could not " in any case " give the powers "the right to interfere, either collectively or separately, in the relations of . . . the Sultan with his subjects, or in the internal administration of his Empire." Articles X.–XIV. renewed the convention of 1841 and neutralized the Black Sea. The waters and ports of this sea, while they were " thrown open to the mercantile marine of every nation," were "formally and in perpetuity interdicted to the flag of war, either of the powers possessing its coasts or of any other power,"[3] except that each of the powers was to be permitted to station two light vessels at the mouths of the Danube, in order to ensure the enforcement of the regulations as to its navigation, while the Czar and the Sultan were allowed each to reserve the right to maintain in

[1] For Stratford Canning's work in bringing about the firman, Lane-Poole, see *Life of Stratford Canning*, vol. ii, chap. xxxii.

[2] The firman is found in Hertslet, vol. ii, p. 1243.

[3] Art. XI.

the Black Sea six steam vessels of not more than 800 tons and
four light steam or sailing vessels of not more than 200 tons.[1]
The Czar and the Sultan also agreed not to establish or maintain
on the coast of the Black Sea "any military-maritime
arsenal."[2]   Articles XV.–XIX. established the free navigation
of the Danube according to the principle of the treaty of
Vienna, and provided for the appointment of commissions to
improve and to regulate the navigation of the river.   Articles
XX.–XXVII. pledged to Moldavia and Wallachia an independent and national administration under the suzerainty of
the Porte and the guarantee of the powers, and stipulated for
a commission to revise the laws and statutes of those principalities.   Portions of Bessarabia were detached from Russia
and united to Moldavia, much to the vexation of the Russian
representative.   Not only was his pride wounded, but he was
specially aggrieved by the efforts of Austria to obtain possession of the territory.   Articles XXVIII.–XXIX. confirmed
Servia in all her special rights and immunities, which were
thenceforth placed under the collective guarantee of the
powers; and, although the Porte was permitted still to maintain its garrison at Belgrade, any armed intervention in Servia
was forbidden without the previous agreement of the powers.

After the settlement of the chief points bearing upon the
Eastern Question, the Congress formulated conclusions upon
certain other matters.   The most important of these was the
declaration respecting Maritime Law.   This act, the object of
which was admitted to be "to introduce into international
relations fixed principles in this respect," and to which the
states not represented in the Congress were, therefore, to be
invited "to accede," declared: " 1. Privateering is, and remains
abolished.   2. The neutral flag covers enemy's goods, with the
exception of contraband of war.   3. Neutral goods, with the
exception of contraband of war, are not liable to capture under

[1] Arts. XIV, XIX, and additional convention of March 30, 1856.
[2] Art. XIII.

enemy's flag.   4. Blockades, in order to be binding, must be
effective, that is to say, maintained by a force sufficient really
to prevent access to the coast of the enemy." [1]   In less than a
year this declaration was adhered to by substantially all civilized states except the United States, Spain and Mexico.   The
United States, however, offered to accede on condition that
private property at sea be altogether exempted from capture
except in case of contraband or of blockade; and the rules of
the declaration, except the first, may be considered as undoubtedly forming to-day a part of international law.

The Congress also adopted a protocol in relation to mediation; [2] but the high expectations which this act seemed at first
to excite as a measure for the prevention of war were doomed
to early and sanguinary disappointment.

Certain other subjects, among which was the Italian question, were considered by the Congress, but they did not get
beyond the pale of discussion.

It was formerly the habit of writers to affirm that the
Crimean war, judged by its results, was a failure, but it is believed that a truer perspective of the history of the day, and a
more impartial estimate of the influence of the conflict on the
later European situation, justify a modification of that judg-
ment.   Some of the provisions of the Treaty of Paris were
undoubtedly diplomatic blunders.   To promise to maintain the
territorial integrity of a state which had been undergoing
decay for a century, and at the same time to renounce all right
of interference in its internal affairs, was to ignore the lessons
of the past and to invite trouble in the future.   No reform had
ever been carried out by the Ottoman Porte except under the
pressure of some outside power, and the man to whom the
Hatti-Humayoun of February 18, 1856, was chiefly due pre-
dicted after the treaty was signed that the charter of reform

[1] Hertslet, vol. ii, p. 1282.

[2] *Ibid.*, vol. ii, p. 1277.

would be a dead letter.[1]   But so far as the war was designed
to prevent the Russian absorption of Turkey, it can hardly be
pronounced a failure.   It is true that Russia re-asserted her
rights on the Black Sea in 1870, and regained Bessarabia in
1878. But after two centuries of almost uninterrupted progress,
she was forced indefinitely to postpone her hope of dominion
over the Ottoman Empire; for Europe had taken Turkey
under its protection, and had made the future of the empire a
matter of common concern.   The war, moreover, wrought a
far-reaching change in the relations between the various European states.   The diplomacy of the period prior to the revolution of 1848 had been directed to the maintenance of the
treaties of 1815, and the same period was marked by the
alliance of the two constitutional states of the West, France
and England, as a counterpoise to the alliance of the absolute
monarchies of the East, Austria, Russia and Prussia.   But the
Crimean War changed all this.   The leadership in Europe
passed from Austria to France, and one of the principal objects
of the reign of Napoleon was the destruction of the system
founded on the treaties of 1815.   After the war, Austria had
not a friend in Europe, but did have, on the other hand, three
persistent enemies, France, Prussia and Sardinia, and she became the object of the machinations of the three men who
were to control the destinies of Europe during the next fifteen
years, Napoleon III., Cavour and Bismarck.   England withdrew from active participation in continental politics during
that period, and turned her attention to home affairs, while
Russia, in order to recover from the losses of the war, was
obliged to devote herself to the improvement of her industries
and finances.

[1] The first words of Stratford Canning at Constantinople when he received the
terms of peace were, " I would rather have cut off my right hand than have signed
that treaty."   Lane-Poole, *Life of Stratford Canning*, vol. ii, chap. xxxii, p. 436.

CHAPTER VII

THE TREATY OF BERLIN

HAD the provisions of the Hatti-Humayoun of February 18, 1856, been carried out, the Ottoman Empire would have been regenerated and would have become a lay state. This celebrated edict provided for perfect religious equality; it opened all positions, civil and military, to Christians; it established mixed tribunals which should publicly administer a new code of laws that was to be drawn up; it guaranteed equality of taxes, did away with the kharadj, decreed the abolition of tax-farming, and provided that Christians should have seats in all provincial boards of administration; and it promised general improvement by the building of roads and canals, and by new methods in the conduct of the finances. Even had the Ottoman Porte been never so well inclined to carry out the provisions of the edict faithfully, almost insuperable difficulties stood in the way. Mohammedan contempt for the infidel was not lessened, and the Turks refused to be associated with Giaours in administration, to recognize their authority in civil and military matters, or to accept their verdicts when they participated in the mixed tribunals. The Christians, on the other hand, preferred to pay an army tax rather than serve in the army; they were afraid to occupy seats in the mixed tribunals or to hold positions of prominence; and the Greek bishops, though they gladly accepted religious equality, objected to relinquishing any of their historic rights, which the Sultan thought should be given up under the new régime. As a matter of fact, it was not long before all attempts to give effect to the edict were abandoned, and things reverted to their former condition. The powers had promised not to interfere, and could, therefore, only protest. Fanaticism increased, and in 1860 the uprising of the Druses against the Maronites in Syria resulted in such massacres that Syria was occupied by French troops.[1] The Ottoman Porte answered the protests of the powers with new promises of reform, and there the matter ended. After the accession of Abdul-Aziz in 1861, a few attempts at improvement were made by the reformers Fuad and Ali, but the opposition of the Old Turk party and the vacillation of the Sultan defeated their efforts. The condition of affairs became so outrageous that the powers instituted an investigation in 1867, and showed in a published memoir that the Hatti-Humayoun of 1856 was practically a dead letter. But the stirring events of 1860–1870 in central Europe to a great extent diverted attention from Turkey, and when the next decade opened the tendency to retrogression continued unchecked.

Meanwhile evidences of disintegration in the empire had been steadily accumulating. A convention was signed August 19, 1858, by the representatives of the powers at Paris, by which it was provided that the principalities of Moldavia and Wallachia should have a common name, the United Principalities; but they were to retain their separate administrations and the Divan of each was to elect its own hospodar.[2] The Roumanians of the two provinces, however, determined to form a united state, and elected the same person, Col. Alexander Couza. The powers yielded before this expression of the national will, and in 1859 recognized the union, as also did the Porte in 1861.[3] But the Roumanians soon discovered that on account of local jealousies, government by one of themselves was not a success; and early in

---

[1] The convention for that purpose is found in Hertslet, *Map of Europe by Treaty*, vol. ii, p. 1455.

[2] *Ibid.*, vol. ii, p. 1329.

[3] *Ibid.*, vol. ii, p. 1377, and *ibid.*, vol. ii, p. 1498.

1866 Couza was compelled to abdicate and Prince Charles of Hohenzollern was called to the throne.[1]   With a single head, a capital, a ministry and an assembly, Roumania, though legally under the suzerainty of the Porte, became practically independent, and recognition of its independence was at length accorded in 1878.

The success of the Roumanians inspired the various Servian nationalities, who hoped to form a great Servian state.   In 1861, the Herzegovinians demanded a national bishop and separate ecclesiastical privileges, and when these were refused by the Sultan they revolted.   They were soon joined by the Montenegrins and Servians, and although the revolt was unsuccessful, the powers compelled the Sultan to withdraw all Turkish troops from Servia except from Belgrade and four fortresses;[2] and in 1867, by friendly agreement, they were withdrawn entirely from Servian territory.[3]   Servia thus became independent in all military and administrative matters, and was also ready for recognition in 1878.

The Cretans, frenzied by the increasing tyranny of the Turks, rose, in 1866, with a view to ultimate annexation to Greece, with whose people they were allied in blood and language. The Greek government and people aided them, and war between Greece and Turkey seemed to be imminent.   But the powers interfered and decided that Crete should remain with Turkey, but that the Sultan should grant a constitution to the Cretans. The Organic Law of 1868 was, therefore, promulgated, but like all the other reforms, it soon became a dead letter.[4]

Egypt also sought to remove the Turkish yoke, but by the use of money rather than of force.   In 1867, the Pasha bought

[1] The protocols of conference between the great Powers relative to the revolution are found in the *British and Foreign State Papers*, vol. lvii, p. 533 *et seq.*

[2] Hertslet, vol. ii, p. 1515.

[3] *Ibia.*, vol. iii, p. 1800.

[4] For the Organic Law of 1868, see *British and Foreign State Papers*, vol. lviii, p. 137.

from the Sultan the title of Khedive and obtained independence in all that concerned customs duties, police, postal and transit affairs.[1]

In Bulgaria the patriotic party, backed up by Russia, obtained from the Sultan, in 1870, the right to have an Exarch of their own and a national church, despite the excommunication of the Greek patriarch of Constantinople.

In 1871, Russia, taking advantage of the Franco-German war, issued a circular note to the various European powers declaring herself to be no longer bound by that part of the Treaty of Paris which imposed disabilities upon her in the Black Sea. The London Conference, while it condemned the method, recognized the fact.[2]

It was evident that affairs in Turkey were fast approaching a crisis, which would result in the revolt of the subject peoples and the interference of the powers, notwithstanding the stipulations of the Treaty of Paris. In 1871, Ali Pasha, the last of the reformers, died and the disorders in the government increased. The subject peoples, crushed by their burdens, were rebellious, and were, moreover, incited to revolt by Slavic sympathizers. At length in July, 1875, the Herzogovinians and Bosniaks rose, and men and money poured to their assistance from Servia and Montenegro. The courts of St. Petersburg, Berlin and Vienna, which had agreed, in 1872, to act in concert on the Eastern Question, warned the Sultan, and on August 18, 1875, demanded that a commission of their consuls should be permitted to proceed to the revolted country, hear the demands of the people and transmit them to Constantinople where they should immediately be acted upon. This was done, and the Sultan, not content with conceding the demands of the insurgents, issued, on the 2nd of October, an iradé, which not

---

[1] *State Papers*, vol. lix, p. 582.

[2] The Russian note is found in Hertslet, vol. iii, p. 1892, and the declaration of the London conference at p. 1904. See also Hall, *International Law*, fourth edition, p. 309 *et seq.*

only granted what they asked, but gave them extensive local privileges besides.[1] Unfortunately for him, the comedy of reform had been played too often; the insurgents ignored his edict and kept on with their struggle.

As in the past, Austria was the power that exhibited the greatest concern at the course of events. To permit the existing condition of affairs to continue would mean either Russian intervention or the formation of a Serb state, either of which would be perilous to the Austro-Hungarian Empire. Count Andrassy, the Austrian chancellor, therefore offered to draw up a note of protest to be signed by the signatories of the Treaty of Paris. England demanded sufficient delay to permit the Sultan to carry out the reforms promised in the iradé of October 2nd; and on December 12th the Sultan issued a second iradé still more munificent than the first, promising the most extensive reforms in judicial, financial and administrative matters.[2] But the Bosniaks and Herzegovinians refused to be conciliated by promises. Andrassay, therefore, submitted his note on the 30th of December to Germany and Russia, by whom it was accepted.[3] It was then sent to London, Paris and Rome. At the two latter capitals it received immediate adherence, and England promised to give it a general support, though she refused to commit herself to any particular action.[4] The European directory therefore appeared to be in accord, and on January 30, 1876, the Andrassy note was sent to the Porte. It demanded that the Turkish government put into execution without delay the following reforms: (1) The establishment of full religious liberty and equality of sects; (2) the abolition of tax-farming; (3) the application of the revenues gathered in Bosnia and Herzegovina entirely to local purposes, and their distribution by local assemblies composed

---

[1] Hertslet, vol. iv, p. 2407.

[2] *Ibid.*, vol. iv, p. 2409.

[3] *Ibid.*, vol. iv, p. 2418.

[4] *Ibid.*, vol. iv, p. 2430.

half of Christians and half of Mussulmans elected by the inhabitants; (4) the amelioration of the condition of the agricultural population. On February 13th the Sultan accepted the note, and a few days later published a new set of promises, relating to the government of the provinces, more elaborate than any that had preceded.[1]

Austria was satisfied with the results of the Andrassy note, and, fearing a sympathetic uprising of the Slavs in her own dominion, employed every effort to check the insurrection and to persuade the insurgents to lay down their arms. The latter, on the contrary, pushed the war more vigorously than before, and Servia and Montenegro began open preparations to come to their aid. Moreover, at the suggestion of Russia, the insurgents drew up early in April a list of the reforms which they demanded should be guaranteed by the European powers. The Russian chancellor, Gortchakoff, proposed to Austria to send the demands to the Porte with a note to the effect that if they were not carried out, the powers would adopt measures to enforce them. Austria declined the proposal; but on May 7th a Mussulman mob in Salonika destroyed the French and German consulates and murdered the consuls. The necessity for action was evident, and on the invitation of Bismarck, Gortchakoff and Andrassy united with him at Berlin in drafting a new note to the Porte. At the suggestion of Gortchakoff, the demands of the insurgents of the month before were made the basis of the note, and on May 13th the conference agreed to the Berlin memorandum.[2] It was much more severe than the Andrassy note. It required that the Sultan (1) rebuild all the houses destroyed in the revolted countries, furnish the peasants with cattle and implements, and exempt them for three years from taxation; (2) establish a Christian commission for the distribution of this aid; (3) withdraw the Turkish troops except in specified

[1] Hertslet, vol. iv, p. 2441 et seq.

[2] Ibid., vol. iv, p. 2459.

places; (4) authorize the Christians to remain armed until the reforms were effected; and (5) delegate to the consuls of the powers the supervision of the execution of the reforms. Moreover, the memorandum demanded that an armistice of two months be granted, and declared that, if at the expiration of that time the desired end had not been accomplished, the powers would resort to efficacious measures "to arrest the evil and prevent its development." The Berlin memorandum was then sent to Paris, Rome and London. At the two former capitals it was immediately accepted, but in London it was rejected without hesitation.[1] Disraeli would accept no plan bearing the stamp of Russian suggestion.

Nevertheless, the other powers decided to send the memorandum to the Porte, and May 30th was fixed as the day, but on the night of the 29th an event occurred which caused the memorandum to be forgotten. An opposition had long existed among the patriotic Turks against Abdul-Aziz because of his indifference to the welfare of his country, and this opposition determined on a revolution. Led by Midhat-Pasha, Young Turkey, as the reformers were called, obtained the necessary Fetva from the Sheik-ul-Islam, deposed Abdul-Aziz and placed his nephew Mourad V. on the throne. The new government immediately adopted a vigorous policy and demanded of Servia the meaning of her extensive war preparations. Servia, believing herself thoroughly prepared for a conflict, demanded in turn that the Turks evacuate Bosnia and Herzogovina and allow the first to be occupied by Servian and the second by Montenegrin troops. The Porte answered with an immediate refusal, and on May 30th Servia, and on July 2nd Montenegro, declared war.[2] To the surprise of Europe the Turks were generally victorious, and overran Servia, upon whom they sought to impose severe terms, comprehending a return to the state of things existing previously to 1867, an

[1] Hertslet, vol. iv, p, 2464.

[2] *Ibid.*, vol. iv, pp. 2471 and 2475.

indemnity for the expenses of the war, and an increase in the amount of the tribute.[1]

Fortunately for Servia, an event had meanwhile taken place which was to result in her salvation. Bulgaria had not been concerned in the general rising of the Slavs of the Ottoman Empire, having been satisfied with the ecclesiastical privileges obtained in 1870 and the reforms introduced by Midhat Pasha. But a small outbreak at Batak, fomented by outsiders, caused the government to send bands of Bashi-Bazouks[2] into the country, all the regular troops being engaged against the rebels elsewhere. During the month of May, the Bashi-Bazouks massacred Christians to a number variously estimated from 12,000 to 25,000, and committed wanton outrages upon the remaining population. The civilized world was horrified at the atrocities as they gradually became known, and England particularly was stirred by the speeches and writings of Mr. Gladstone. When, therefore, in August, 1876, Servia appealed to the powers to mediate with the Turks, and the powers referred her petition to Great Britain as the government whose advice the Porte was most likely to take, Disraeli did not dare openly to refuse to act as mediator. In September, he proposed an armistice of six weeks, the maintenance of the status quo ante bellum in Servia, and a certain amount of administrative independence for Bosnia, Herzegovina and Bulgaria.[3] But Young Turkey was determined to settle the affairs of the empire without the tutelage of Europe. On August 31st, the leaders of the party deposed Mourad V., who was an imbecile, and elevated in his stead Abdul-Hamid II., who though ignorant and inexperienced, was energetic and full of zeal for the defense of his faith. Instead of answering the proposal of Great Britain, the new government issued an extraordinary edict of reform, which was to change Turkey into a modern

[1] Hertslet, vol. iv, p. 2482.

[2] The Bashi-Bazonks were irregulars drafted from the heart of Asia Minor.

[3] Hertslet, vol. iv, p. 2488.

constitutional state. There was to be a responsible ministry,
an assembly of two chambers, freedom of speech and of the
press, permanent judges and compulsory education. The
Turkish government, moreover, demanded that the armistice
should be extended to six months, and that during that time
the revolted provinces, as well as Servia and Montenegro,
should receive no aid from without. Its apparent design was
to employ the interval in improving its own forces.

The patience of the Czar was now exhausted. Alexander II.
was himself a lover of peace, but the bureaucrats who surrounded him were strong for war with Turkey, and they were
supported by the Russian people, who demanded the protection
of their co-religionists in the Ottoman Empire. In the previous July, Alexander had met Francis Joseph at Reichstadt,
where it is generally assumed that he obtained the consent of
the latter to Russian intervention in case Turkey should refuse the demands of the powers, provided that, in the event of
Bulgaria's liberation, Bosnia and Herzegovina should be given
to Austria.[1] At all events Austria appeared to take less interest in the war after the interview. The Czar was also sure
of the neutrality of Germany, for Bismarck was known to hold
the opinion which he afterwards avowed that the Eastern
question was not worth to Germany the bones of a single Pom-
eranian grenadier. On October 15th, Alexander sent Gen.
Ignatieff to Constantinople with full powers to agree upon the
following terms: (1) An armistice of six weeks without reserve; (2) autonomy for Bosnia, Herzegovina and Bulgaria;
(3) a guarantee of their rights by Europe. The Turks pro-
crastinated, and at the same time pushed the war in Servia so
vigorously that by October 30th the road to Belgrade was entirely open to them. The moment the news reached Ignatieff
he sent in the Russian ultimatum—the acceptance of the armis-

---

[1] Bismarck distinctly states in his *Autobiography*, vol. ii, chap. xxviii, p. 235,
that such an agreement was made.

tice in forty-eight hours or war. The Porte, overawed, immediately yielded, and the armistice began November 2d.[1]

The action of the Czar aroused the suspicions of English
statesmen, notwithstanding that Alexander had assured Lord
Loftus, the British ambassador, that Russia desired no conquest or territorial aggrandizement.[2] Gladstone fell from
favor and Disraeli once more became popular. On November
9th, at the Lord Mayor's banquet, Disraeli declared that if a
war broke out, no country was better prepared for it than
England, and that she would not hesitate to undertake it.
But Lord Derby, then minister for foreign affairs, who
accepted the friendly words of Alexander in good faith, had
on November 4th proposed the holding of a conference at
Constantinople to consider the Eastern Question; and the
proposition was accepted by all the powers.[3] Lord Salisbury
was chosen as the delegate of England, and on his way to the
Turkish capital he stopped at Berlin, where he represented to
Bismarck that it was advisable to give the Porte more time to
carry out its reforms, and that, if it should afterwards become
necessary to employ coercive measures, they should be undertaken by Europe, and not alone by Russia. Lord Salisbury,
however, received little comfort from the German chancellor.[4]
The preliminary sessions of the conference were held on the
11th to the 22d of December, and were marked by the mutual
opposition of the British and Russian representatives. On
December 24th, the Ottoman Porte was invited to send a
delegate to sit at the formal sessions, which were about to be
occupied with the conditions agreed upon during the preliminary meetings. These conditions[5] included an increase

---

[1] Hertslet, vol. iv, pp. 2502, 2504.

[2] Lord Loftus to the Earl of Derby, Hertslet, vol. iv, p. 2506.

[3] Hertslet, vol. iv, p. 2516.

[4] Salisbury's instructions are found in vol. 68, p. 1064, of the *British and Foreign State Papers*.

[5] Hertslet, vol. iv, p. 2541; *State Papers*, vol. lxviii, p. 1114.

of territory for Servia and Montenegro, and autonomy for
Bosnia, Herzegovina and Bulgaria, which were to enjoy the
right to have a national militia, and to use the national language in official acts, and were to be occupied by Belgian
troops until the accomplishment of reforms under an international commission.

During the discussions the conditions underwent certain
modifications favorable to Turkey, and as thus modified they
were on January 15, 1877, formally presented to the Porte.
But, on the 23d of the preceding December, the new constitution of Turkey had been proclaimed with elaborate cere-
monies,[1] and when the powers presented their conditions, the
Turkish government answered that it was impossible to accept
them, (1) because they were a menace to the independence of
the Sultan, (2) because they were in violation of the Treaty of
Paris, and (3) because they were contrary to the new constitution. The delegates of the powers then quitted Constantinople on January 20th, and Abdul-Hamid II., as though to
show the worthlessness of his constitutional reforms, on
February 5th dismissed and disgraced the man who had
instigated them—Midhat Pasha. On January 31st, Gortchakoff invited the powers to make known what measures they
intended to employ to bring the Porte to reason, and he let it
be understood that the Czar was resolved to act alone, if
necessary.[2] At the end of February, Gen. Ignatieff was sent
to the various European capitals to request that, if the various
powers would not unite with Russia in requiring the Porte to
accept the programme which it had rejected, they would
permit Russia to proceed alone. The general was well received at all the capitals except London. There Lord Derby
insisted upon one more concerted effort to bring Turkey to
terms. A conference was opened at London, with representatives of all the great powers present; and on March 31st they

[1] The Constitution is found in Hertslet, vol. iv, p. 2531.

[2] *State Papers*, vol. lxviii, p. 1104.

agreed to a protocol,[1] the principal features of which were a demand that the Porte should really put into execution the reforms so often promised, and a statement to the effect that the powers proposed, through their representatives at Constantinople and their consuls in the various localities, to watch carefully how the reforms were applied. The London protocol was presented to the Sultan on April 3d, and he transmitted it to his make-believe parliament, by which it was rejected April 9th.[2] The Porte notified the powers two days later that Turkey was making its own reforms, and as an independent state could not submit to outside interference. April 16th the Czar concluded a convention with Roumania for unobstructed passage through her territory ;[3] and on the 24th of the month he proclaimed war against Turkey,[4] declaring that he did so without any ambitious designs, and merely for the purpose of succoring the oppressed Christians of the Ottoman Empire. The Porte invoked article VIII. of the Treaty of Paris, which provided that in case of a conflict between Turkey and another state, the great powers should try their friendly mediation ;[5] but the good old days of 1856 were gone. Every power except England soon declared its neutrality, and England was by no means a unit in supporting the bellicose policy of Disraeli. England also finally declared her neutrality, April 30th, 1877,[6] on condition that the Czar should not interfere with Egypt or the Suez Canal, and above all should not occupy Constantinople.[7] Gortchakoff assented to these conditions, with the reservation that the exigencies of war

[1] Hertslet, vol. iv, p. 2563.

[2] *Ibid.*, vol. iv, p. 2568.

[3] *Ibid.*, vol. iv, p. 2576 *et seq.*

[4] *Ibid.*, vol. iv, p. 2598.

[5] *Ibid.*, vol. iv, p. 2598.

[6] *State Papers*, vol. lxviii, p. 859.

[7] Hertslet, vol. iv, p. 2615.

might demand the temporary occupation of the city.[1] Lord
Derby replied that in case of such occupation England would
consider herself free to take whatever measures of precaution
might seem to be necessary.[2]

Immediately after the declaration of war, the Russian troops
crossed the Turkish frontier both in Europe and in Asia, but
the bad roads and high waters and the poor administration of
the military service prevented their reaching the Danube till
the end of June. Once across the river they forced the pass-
ages of the Balkans, and by the end of July they occupied
Hermanli, only two days march from Adrianople. In Asia
they were equally successful, and in May the fortress of Kars,
the key to the Turkish Asiatic dominions, was besieged.
These rapid achievements astonished Europe and caused the
greatest apprehension at London and Vienna. Disraeli ordered the English fleet to Besika Bay, and Andrassy began
the mobilization of the Austrian troops. But the tide of war
soon changed. Osman Pasha, the Turkish commander, in-
trenched himself at Plevna in front of the main body of the
Russian army and stopped all further advance; Suleiman
Pasha drove the right wing of the Russian army back across
the Balkans, and in Asia the Russians were compelled to raise
the siege of Kars and beat a general retreat. By the opening
of November the Turks apparently were masters of the situation. But the Russians were goaded by these blows into put
ting forth the greatest exertions. Todleben, the hero of
Sebastopol, was sent to supervise the siege of Plevna.
Roumania, who had concluded on May 14th an offensive and
defensive alliance with Russia, hurried forward an army corps
which did excellent service,[3] and Servia broke the peace which
she had signed on March 1st, and put her armies in motion.[4]

[1] Hertslet, vol. iv, pp. 2624–34.
[2] *Ibid.*, vol. iv, p. 2646.
[3] *Ibid.*, vol. iv, p. 2618.
[4] The Servian Declaration of War is found in Hertslet, vol. iv, p. 2468.

The resources of the Turks were overtaxed, and the fortunes of war once more shifted. Kars was taken in Asia; Suleiman Pasha was defeated in Bulgaria, and finally on December 10th, after one of the most heroic defenses known in history, Plevna surrendered to Todleben. The Russians immediately pushed across the Balkans, massed the main army at Adrianople and established two posts on the Sea of Marmora. Constantinople was at their mercy.

The Ottoman Porte hastened to solicit the collective mediation of the great powers. But this was unattainable without the concurrence of Germany, and Bismarck would not interfere. On January 3, 1878, the Porte therefore agreed to treat with Russia alone. Meanwhile, all the old-time distrust of Russia had revived in England, and the war-party had steadily been gaining ground. Disraeli maintained that the affairs of the Orient could not be settled without the agreement of the signatories of the treaties of 1856 and 1871.[1] The Russians worked to gain time, and prolonged negotiations with the Porte till their troops were at the very gates of Constantinople. On January 30th an armistice and preliminaries of peace were signed at Adrianople.[2] When the powers inquired as to the terms of the preliminaries, Gortchakoff replied that their basis was the independence of Roumania and Servia, an increase of territory for Montenegro, autonomy for Bosnia, Herzegovina and Bulgaria, and the payment of a war indemnity to Russia. It was not improbable that the terms thus vaguely announced would be hardened in the definitive treaty. So at least thought Andrassy and Beaconsfield. On February 3rd Austria, indignant at the disposal of Bosnia and Herzegovina in a manner contrary to what was believed to be the promise of the Czar in the previous July, notified Russia that she would consider null any agreement between the belligerents which should modify existing treaties and which should affect the

---

[1] See memorandum to Gortchakoff in Hertslet, voi. iv, p. 257.

[2] Hertslet, vol. iv, p. 2661.

interests of Europe, and especially those of Austria-Hungary, unless it were submitted to a conference of the powers ; and she suggested that such a conference should meet at Vienna.[1] As to Beaconsfield, he went a step further, and on February 15th ordered the English fleet with troops on board to pass the Dardanelles and anchor in front of Constantinople. The Czar then promised that if the English would abstain from landing troops, his forces would not enter the city.[2] Gortchakoff had answered the note of Andrassy evasively, demanding that a distinction be made between what in the treaty affected all Europe and that which concerned only Russia and Turkey. At the same time he treated with Bismarck, who had up to this time been favorable to Russia, for the opening of a congress at Berlin, and on the 3d of March Bismarck invited the powers to send representatives to such a congress.

On the very day that Bismarck took this step, the definitive treaty of San Stefano was signed.[3] By its terms Turkey was required to recognize the independence of Roumania, Servia and Montenegro, all of which were to be increased in size. But the most important stipulation was that for the erection of the autonomous tributary principality of Bulgaria, with a Christian government and a national militia, and with boundaries extending from the Black Sea on the east to Albania on the west, and from the Danube on the north to the Ægean on the south. This would have practically blotted out Turkey as a European power. What was left was to be divided into four parts unconnected with each other : The environs of Constantinople on the east, the peninsula of Salonika in the south, Thessaly and Albania in the west and southwest, and Bosnia, Herzegovina and Novi Bazar in the northwest. The prince of Bulgaria, who was not to be a member of any of the reigning dynasties of the great European powers, was to be elected by the

[1] Hertslet, vol. iv, p. 2668.

[2] *Ibid.*, vol. iv, p. 2670.

[3] *Ibid.*, vol. iv, p. 2672 *et seq.*

the people, and confirmed by the Porte, with the assent of the powers; but the constitution of the principality was to be drawn up by an assembly of Bulgarian notables under the supervision of a Russian commissioner, who was to superintend the administration of affairs for two years, supported by 50,000 Russian troops. Bosnia and Herzegovina were to receive the reforms demanded for them at the conference of Constantinople, with such modifications as might be agreed upon by the Porte, Russia and Austria-Hungary. The Porte engaged to apply to Crete the Organic Law of 1868, to extend analogous reforms to the other Greek provinces of the Empire, and to improve the condition of Armenia, and guarantee the safety of the inhabitants from the Kurds and Circassians. Turkey also assumed to pay a war indemnity of 1,410,000,000 rubles, but the Czar, in view of the " financial embarrassment " of Turkey, agreed to commute 1,100,000,000 rubles for territory in Asia, and for the Sandjak of Tultcha, which Roumania was to be obliged to take in exchange for that part of Bessarabia which was detached from Russia in 1856, and which was now to be restored to her. Russian ecclesiastics, pilgrims and monks traveling or sojourning in the Ottoman Empire, together with their property and establishments, were placed under the official protection of the Czar, and priests and others in holy places, and especially the monks of Mt. Athos, of Russian origin, were confirmed in their privileges. The Straits were to be always open to the merchant ships of the world, and the old treaties of commerce between the two countries were to be maintained.

There were two states that were determined to prevent the carrying out of the treaty of San Stefano—Austria-Hungary and England. The latter took immediate action. March 13th Lord Derby notified Bismarck that England would not send a representative to the congress at Berlin unless the treaty of San Stefano should be considered in its entirety. After two weeks of spirited correspondence between London and St.

Petersburg, the Czar announced on March 26th his refusal to submit to the congress those portions of the treaty which concerned only Russia and Turkey. Both countries began to sound the other powers. In France the Duc Decazes, supported by the Royalists, who were friendly to Russia, had just been driven from office, and M. Waddington, who was known to be friendly to England, succeeded him in charge of foreign affairs. Austria-Hungary naturally supported England. Italy, who had hoped for something on the Albanian coast, did likewise. There remained only Germany, who, before and during the war, had given to Russia a friendly support. But Gortchakoff was now to be grievously disappointed, for Bismarck gave his approval to the plan of laying the entire treaty before the proposed congress. Under such circumstances, Beaconsfield felt justified in defying Russia. On March 28th he allowed Lord Derby to resign from the foreign office, and replaced him with Lord Salisbury. He then reinforced the British fleet before Constantinople, and sent additional troops to Malta, and on April 1st Lord Salisbury notified Europe [1] that the treaty of San Stefano placed the Black Sea under the absolute domination of Russia, destroyed the real independenee of the Ottoman Empire, and was in general contrary to the interests of Great Britain. Russia, weakened by war and diplomatically isolated, could only submit, and on April 9th Gortchakoff, incensed at what he considered his betrayal by Bismarck, addressed a note to London asking for the modifications which England would demand in the treaty.[2] They were communicated to Count Shuvaloff, then Russian ambassador at London, who bore them to St. Petersburg, where they were accepted by the Czar. Shuvaloff immediately returned to London and signed the secret treaty of May 31st, which provided for almost all the important modifications which we shall soon see were made in the treaty of San

[1] Hertslet, vol. iv, p. 2698.

[2] *Ibid.*, vol. iv, p. 2707.

Stefano. While this transaction was in progress, Beaconsfield was negotiating with the Porte for the cession of the island of Cyprus, in return for which Great Britain was to defend the Turkish possessions in Asia Minor against Russia, the Porte promising to introduce into those possessions reforms which were to be agreed upon later between the two powers. A treaty to this effect was secretly signed June 4th.[1]

The Congress of Berlin opened its sessions on June 13, 1878, and exactly one month later the Treaty of Berlin was signed. The chief figures at the congress were Beaconsfield and Salisbury, who appeared for England; Gortchakoff and Shuvaloff, for Russia; Bismarck, who was president of the Congress, for Germany; Andrassy, for Austria, and Waddington, for France. Italy and Turkey, and when their interests were in question, Greece and Roumania, were also represented. The twenty sittings of the Congress formed one continuous struggle between the representatives of England and Russia. Germany and Austria almost always, and France and Italy usually, supported England, and on almost every important question the Russian representatives found themselves alone. Gortchakoff never forgave Bismarck for his attitude at the Congress,[2] and as the sessions continued, and the treatment of the Slavic cause at the hands of the Germans and Magyars became known, there sprang up in Russia an intensely angry feeling, not so much against England, from whom Russia expected nothing, as against Germany, from whom she expected much.

By the Treaty of Berlin, as signed July 13, 1878,[3] the Bulgarian principality erected by the treaty of San Stefano was divided into three parts: (1) Bulgaria proper, which was to

---

[1] Hertslet, vol. iv, p. 2722.

[2] For Bismarck's view as to the causes of Gortchakoff's enmity, see chaps. xxviii and xxix of his Autobiography.

[3] The protocols of the Congress may be found in the *State Papers*, vol. 9, p. 82. Abstracts are given in Hertslet, vol. iv, pp. 2729 *et seq.* The treaty is given in English in Hertslet, vol. iv, pp. 2759 *et seq.*

extend from the Danube to the Balkans, and which was to become an autonomous principality, and to pay an annual tribute to the Sultan; the prince, who was not to be a member of the reigning dynasties of the great powers, to be elected by the people and confirmed by the Porte, with the assent of the powers. (2) Eastern Roumelia, a name invented to designate southern Bulgaria, which was to have an autonomous administration and a Christian governor-general appointed by the Sultan for five years with the assent of the powers, but was to remain under the political and military control of the Porte. (3) Macedonia, which was given back without reserve to the Sultan. This division reduced the new principality, as it was constituted under the Treaty of San Stefano, by more than one-half, both in territory and in population, and removed it, and incidentally Russian influence, entirely from the Ægean Bosnia and Herzegovina were placed under the control of Austria-Hungary for an indeterminate period, and the same power was also authorized to keep garrisons and have military and commercial roads in the Sandjak of Novi-Bazar, privileges which placed her on the road to Salonika, the goal of her ambition. The Turkish representatives protested vigorously against this action, which displeased Servia and Montenegro also; but the congress was obdurate. Servia and Montenegro were recognized as independent principalities, but received only slight accessions of territory, instead of the large increases allowed them by the treaty of San Stefano. To Greece nothing was given; but the treaty provided for direct negotiations between Turkey and Greece under the supervision of the powers, which resulted in 1881 in her securing Thessaly. The Greek representatives had demanded Albania, Epirus and Crete; but all these were left to Turkey, though it was stipulated that the Organic Law of 1868 should be applied to Crete. Roumania was treated harshly; for, although her independence was recognized, she not only was not compensated for her sacrifices in the war, but was compelled to restore to Russia the detached portion of Bessarabia, a fertile country inhabited by Roumans, receiving in exchange the Dobrudja, inhabited chiefly by Tartars backward in civilization. Religious disabilities were done away with, and freedom of religion and of worship provided for in the new Slavic states, as well as in the Ottoman Empire; ecclesiastics, pilgrims and monks of all nationalities were to enjoy the same rights and privileges in that empire, and were, together with their establishments, to be under the official protection of the diplomatic and consular agents of the powers, though the special rights of France in the Holy Places were to be respected. Russia, besides receiving Bessarabia in Europe, obtained a large part of Armenia and of neighboring districts in Asia; but it was agreed that the reforms to be instituted in Armenia should be applied under the superintendence of the powers, and not, as by the treaty of San Stefano, under that of Russia alone. Two days after the settlement of the Russian claims in Asia was made, England disclosed her secret treaty with Turkey, and announced that she would immediately take possession of Cyprus. To Gortchakoff this was a stunning blow. He had seen Beaconsfield succeed at almost every point, and he pointedly asked the congress to make known the principle and the methods according to which it designed to insure the execution of its august decrees. The last three days of the congress were consumed in a passionate discussion of this question, and then at the suggestion of Lord Salisbury it was dropped. The Russian chancellor went back to St. Petersburg greatly humiliated, while Beaconsfield returned back to London bringing "Peace with Honor," to receive the plaudits of his countrymen.

The work of the Congress of Berlin was not calculated to increase friendliness among the powers of Europe. Turkey felt outraged at being despoiled, not only by her enemy Russia, but by her professed friends, England and Austria The states of the Balkans found their high hopes all dashed to the ground. Roumania complained of the loss of Bessarabia;

Servia and Montenegro, of the disposal of Bosnia and Herzegovina; and Greece, of the scant attention paid to the aspira-
tions cherished by her people. Russia deeply resented the
attitude assumed by the Germans and Magyars toward the
Slavs. Indeed, so violent was the manifestation of feeling in
Russia against Germany and Austria-Hungary that Bismarck
deemed it prudent to form an alliance with the latter power in
October, 1879, for mutual protection, an alliance which was
joined by Italy in 1882, because of the colonial activity of
France in northern Africa. It is only with the lapse of years
and the development of new interests that the ill-feeling engendered at Berlin in 1878 has faded away.

CHAPTER VIII

PRESENT STATUS OF THE EASTERN QUESTION

GREECE, Roumania, and Servia had been successively torn away from all connection with the Ottoman Empire. But the process of disintegration did not end with the treaty of Berlin. The diplomats at the congress, fearful of the erection of a great Bulgarian state under the protectorate of Russia, had, as we have seen, divided Bulgaria, and given to the southern part a new name—Eastern Roumelia. The Russians organized Bulgaria proper, gave it a constitution,[1] filled its official positions, officered its militia and obtained from the new assembly the election as prince of the Czar's candidate, Alexander of Battenberg. The prince at first was pro-Russian, and for four years was involved in conflict with the assembly, which was nationalist and anti-Russian, and demanded the annexation of Eastern Roumelia. September 18, 1883, Prince Alexander, wearied with the insolence and arrogance of the Russians, answered the address of the assembly praying for the restoration of the constitution, which he had suspended in 1881, by immediately granting its request. The Russians then withdrew in resentment from all official positions. In the meantime, Eastern Roumelia had been organized[2] as a self-governing province with a Christian governor, an elective assembly, and a national militia. But the people longed to be united with their brethren of Bulgaria, and on

---

[1] The Constitution is found in full in *State Papers*, vol. 70, p. 1303. Abstract in Hertslet, vol. iv, p. 2866 *et seq*.

[2] The Organic Statute for Eastern Roumelia is found in *State Papers*, vol. 70, p. 759. Abstract in Hertslet, vol. iv, p. 2860.

September 1885, assembly, militia, officials and people rose in rebellion, imprisoned the governor and the commander of the forces, and declared themselves united to Bulgaria. Prince Alexander was aware that the Czar, who was already displeased at the Bulgarians, would feel deeply aggrieved if the union was consummated; but he deemed it better to break with Russia than with his own people, and on September 20th he assumed the title of Prince of the two Bulgarias, and occupied Eastern Roumelia with his army.[1]

The Sultan immediately protested against this violation of the Treaty of Berlin, but the state of affairs at Constantinople and in Crete prevented action. Greece and Servia, however, who were both anxious to extend their own boundaries, at once prepared for war. The powers restrained Greece by blockading her coasts,[2] but Servia declared war November 15th.[3] The Bulgarians were dependent on their own resources, the Russian officers having left their army; but they defeated the Servians at Slivnitza, and although they obtained neither indemnity nor additional territory in the treaty which followed,[4] they secured the union of the two Bulgarias.

The powers held a conference at Constantinople in November, 1885, to consider this violation of the Treaty of Berlin, and Russia demanded that the union be disregarded and annulled; but she was opposed by England, who had changed her policy with regard to the Balkan state since 1878. Though the powers were unwilling to depart from the letter of the Treaty of Berlin, they accepted a compromise[5] to which the Porte had become a party, viz., the appointment by the Sultan of Alexander as governor of Eastern Roumania, a device which did not conceal the real union of the two Bulgarias. Since

[1] *Annual Register*, 1885.

[2] Hertslet, vol. iv, p. 3158 *et seq.*

[3] *Ibid.*, vol. iv, p. 3141.

[4] *Ibid.*, vol. iv, p. 3151.

[5] *Ibid.*, vol, iv, p. 3152.

the union the Bulgarians have shown a remarkable · aptitude for sound politics, and their country has made great progress in economic and social development. The dependence on Turkey is merely nominal; the principality being virtually independent.

Abdul Hamid II. devoted himself in the years following 1878, to carrying out the main provisions of the Treaty of Berlin. He displayed unexpected energy, and in 1884 took the control of affairs out of the hands of the viziers and divan ; and he has since personally conducted the government. Although there had been occasional disorders, the empire had enjoyed a decade of comparative peace when in 1889 outbreaks occurred in Armenia and in Crete. We have seen that by the treaty of San Stefano and then by the treaty of Berlin, the Porte had promised to introduce reforms in Armenia and to protect the inhabitants;[1] and the duty of seeing that the promise was kept seemed especially to rest upon England by reason of the Cyprus convention. Though nothing had been done towards fulfilling the promise, the Armenians during the years of peace after 1878 had themselves improved their condition, and both in their own province, and in the various cities of the Empire where they were scattered, they had become quite prosperous. This brought upon them increased demands of the tax-collectors, which resulted in 1889–1890 in bloody conflicts. At the same time the Armenians formed a national party and demanded autonomous government. The Porte condemned the leaders of the movement as rebels and incited the mountain Kurds to commit outrages upon the Armenians. The latter retaliated, and a state of war soon developed. In November, 1894, a commission appointed by England, France, and Russia, which sat in the troubled country, drew up a scheme of reform,[2] but this only served to render more intense the antagonism between the races; and

[1] *Treaty of Berlin*, Article lxi.

[2] *Annual Register*, 1895.

in 1895–1896 there occurred the massacres which seem to
have been designed to Islamize the Armenians or else to
destroy them. The European powers protested, and in England urgent demands were made upon the government to
interfere. But Russia let it be known that she objected to the
creation of another Bulgaria in Asia Minor; if Turkish Armenia was endowed with autonomy, then Russian Armenia
would want it, and the next demand would be for union. As
Russia was supported by France, Austria and Germany, England could do nothing. In order to compel the powers to act,
a number of Armenian revolutionists attacked the Ottoman
Bank in Constantinople in August, 1896. The government
immediately ordered a massacre of the Armenians in Constantinople, and the order was carried out; but the powers
could come to no agreement in the matter, and nothing was
done.[1]

Crete had been in a state of unrest since the signing of the
Treaty of Berlin. The Cretans had expected that the congress
would unite them to Greece, and were sorely disappointed at
the outcome. Outbreaks began in 1885 which culminated in
1889 in a revolt for autonomy, but the Turkish government
was able to repress it. In 1894, however, a new revolt took
place, and this time the demand was not merely for autonomy,
but for independence and annexation to Greece. The Cretans
progressed so far as to set up a provisional government in
August, 1896, but the powers intervened and brought about a
cessation of hostilities by requiring the Sultan to appoint a
Christian governor and institute reforms.[2] In the meantime
the war fever had spread all over Greece; the government
massed its troops along the Macedonian frontier and sent war-
ships to Crete; but the Greek forces were prevented from
landing in Crete by the fleets of the powers. The Greeks
were enraged at the intervention of the powers and raids were

[1] *Annual Register*, 1896.

[2] *Ibid.*, 1896.

made across the border into Macedonia. The Turkish government on April 18, 1897, then declared war, and in a month had completely defeated the Greeks. The latter were compelled to accept the mediation of the powers, to agree to autonomy for Crete, and to rectify their frontier to the advantage of Turkey.[1] The powers had great difficulty in selecting a governor for Crete, but finally agreed upon Prince George of Greece. The ultimate absorption of Crete by Greece is perhaps only a matter of time.

In 1878, the Egyptian government became bankrupt, and France and England established a condomimum or dual control over the government in order to take care of its finances.[2] The Khedive Ismail during the next year endeavored to get rid of this control. He was deposed by the two powers, and Tewfik Pasha, who was elevated in his stead, showed himself so complaisant to the wishes of the intervenors that an insurrection was raised, in 1881, by Arabi Pasha with the cry of " Egypt for the Egyptians." The representatives of the powers gathered at Constantinople to consider the crisis, but nothing was accomplished; and as France refused to unite with her, England sent a fleet to Alexandria which bombarded the city. Troops were then landed and Arabi was defeated, and the English took practical control of the government in September, 1881.[3] Turkey and France protested, but although England assured the powers that she intended to keep her troops in Egypt only until peace and order were restored, they are there still. October 24, 1885, a convention was signed between Great Britain and Turkey which provided for the sending of a British and a Turkish High Commissioner, who were to take measures for the tranquilization of the country, to re-organize the army and to reform the administration.[4] Since

[1] *Annual Register*, 1897.
[2] *Ibid.*, 1878, p. 347 *et seq*
[3] *Ibid.*, 1882, p. 359 *et seq.*
[4] Hertslet, vol. iv, p. 3274.

that time the English have re-organized the judicial and administrative systems, and although they have declined to declare a protectorate over Egypt, they practically control the country, which is now but nominally bound to the Porte.

The question of the further dismemberment of Turkey is an open one. The small states of the Balkans—Servia, Bulgaria and Greece—have their eyes covetously fixed upon Macedonia. But they are checked in their ambitions by Russia and Austria. Austria, by the extension of her railroads and the conclusion of commercial treaties, has undoubtedly increased her sphere of influence in the direction of Salonika, upon which her gaze has long been fastened. Russia has relinquished her former plan of settling the Balkan question by the establishment of independent nationalities, and adheres for the time being to the maintenance of the territorial integrity of the Ottoman Empire. As a result her influence at Constantinople during the past decade has been very high, while England, once all-powerful, has often seen her suggestions rejected there, as notably in respect of Armenia. As a matter of fact the attitude of the various Powers on the Turkish question is no longer determined by political conditions in Europe, but by colonial and commercial rivalry in Asia and Africa. The Turk in the meanwhile, enjoying increased security, has reorganized his army with the aid of German officers, has to a great extent re-established his financial credit, and by his rapid successes in the Greek war, which has greatly increased his prestige, has apparently assured himself of an indefinite stay at Constantinople.